W9-BJM-635

Steve Jobs

· Business Leaders ·

Steve Jobs

Jim Corrigan

MORGAN
REYNOLDS
PUBLISHING

Greensboro, North Carolina

Business Leaders
Steve Jobs
Copyright © 2013 by Morgan Reynolds Publishing

Library of Congress Cataloging-in-Publication Data

Corrigan, Jim.
  Business leaders : Steve Jobs / by Jim Corrigan.
       p. cm.
  Includes bibliographical references and index.
  ISBN 978-1-59935-076-9
 1. Jobs, Steven, 1955- 2. Computer industry--United States--
Biography. 3. Businesspeople--United States--Biography. 4.
Computer engineers--United States--Biography. I. Title. II. Title:
Steve Jobs.
 HD9696.2.U62J634 2007
 338.7'6100416092--dc22
 [B]

                                       2007039052

Printed in the United States of America
First Edition

Book cover and interior designed by:
Ed Morgan, navyblue design studio
Greensboro, NC

TABLE OF CONTENTS

ONE   Growing Up in Silicon Valley   7

TWO   The Seeds of Apple   21

THREE   Growing Pains   37

FOUR   The NeXT Mistakes   51

FIVE   Pixar Shows Promise   63

SIX   Return to Glory   77

SEVEN   iPod and Beyond   91

EIGHT   Final Years   105

Timeline   118
Sources   120
Bibliography   123
Web sites   124
Index   125

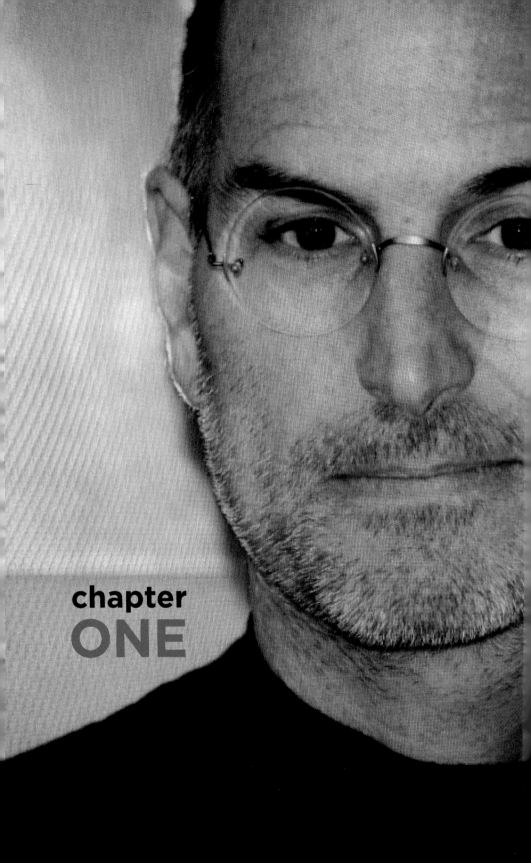

chapter
ONE

GROWING UP IN SILICON VALLEY

"Your time is limited, so don't waste it living someone else's life. . . . Don't let the noise of others' opinions drown out your own inner voice. And most important, have the courage to follow your heart and intuition. They somehow already know what you truly want to become. Everything else is secondary."
—Stanford University commencement address, June 2005

Steve Jobs looked out over the sea of young faces assembled before him. He was standing behind a podium at California's Stanford University, addressing the graduating class of 2005. It was a defining moment for Jobs, who had dropped out of college to become a leader of the computer revolution. At age fifty, Jobs had already climbed the highest peaks—and fallen to the deepest lows—of American business, only to find himself back on top again.

Jobs told the young graduates about important lessons he had learned in life. He talked about being an adopted child. He described the thrill of starting Apple Computer with a friend in his parents' garage. He spoke of his battle with cancer and how it had given him a new outlook on life. He urged the graduates to find the work that they love and to always question conventional wisdom. Jobs concluded with a cherished maxim from his hippie-culture youth: Stay Hungry. Stay Foolish.

Jobs gives the commencement speech at Stanford University in 2005

The Stanford commencement address revealed a rarely glimpsed side of Steve Jobs. He spoke with great passion and conviction, but that was not at all unusual. The difference at Stanford was the content of his speech. He was speaking about himself and the things that mattered to him personally. To be sure, Steve Jobs never eschewed the limelight—in fact, he thrived on it. But most often, he was describing a revolutionary new product, or sharing his vision of the future of technology. For the intensely private Steve Jobs to discuss publicly his personal feelings and motivations was most uncommon.

Steve Jobs's life began on February 24, 1955, in San Francisco, California, a region he would call home for most of his life. He was born to a young, unwed graduate student. The woman had decided while pregnant that she could not keep her baby but was nevertheless concerned about his future. She put the child up for adoption but stipulated that the adoptive parents must be college graduates. A successful attorney and his wife initially agreed to take the baby, but at the last moment they changed their minds. They wanted a girl instead.

The adoption agency scrambled to find a new couple, quickly settling on Paul and Clara Jobs. The Jobses were thrilled by the prospect of adopting the baby boy, but there was a problem—they were not college graduates. Paul Jobs was a Coast Guard veteran who repaired automobiles and other machinery. Clara Jobs was a payroll clerk. The young mother initially refused to sign the adoption papers, agreeing only after the Jobses promised that her child would someday attend college. The couple gave their new son the name Steven Paul Jobs.

As a child, Steve had a reputation as a loner and a troublemaker. He had little interest in schoolwork or sports, but he was eager to learn how machines worked. His father encouraged this natural curiosity. Jobs later recalled:

> He had a workbench out in his garage where, when I was about five or six, he sectioned off a little piece of it and said "Steve, this is your workbench now." And he gave me some of his smaller tools and showed me how to use a hammer and saw and how to build things. It really was very good for me. He spent a lot of time with me . . . teaching me how to build things, how to take things apart, put things back together.

At school, Steve often found himself in trouble. Although he was obviously very intelligent, he loved practical jokes and other antics, and his unruly behavior disrupted the class. His fourth-grade teacher, Mrs. Hill, suspected that Steve was bored with school, so she approached Steve with an advanced math workbook and told him that if he completed it on his own, she would reward him with a five-dollar bill and a giant lollipop.

The challenge worked. It motivated Steve to push himself to learn difficult concepts, and once he got started, he could not stop. He learned so much that by the end of the year his teachers felt that Steve should skip a grade and advance to middle school. "I'm 100 percent sure that if it hadn't been for Mrs. Hill in fourth grade and a few others, I would have absolutely have ended up in jail," Jobs said many years later.

Unfortunately, his academic progress once again faltered in junior high school. The work was more challenging, and there were many tough, streetwise delinquents whose threatening behavior made Steve's discipline problems seem mild by comparison. After struggling through a difficult year, Steve flatly announced to his parents that under no circumstances would he

return to that school. His ultimatum put Paul and Clara Jobs in a bind. They could not afford the tuition of a private school, so their only alternative would be to relocate to a new school district. They packed up the family—which now included an adopted daughter, Patty, who was two years younger than Steve—and moved to a new home. The family's new residence was in the heart of an area soon to be dubbed Silicon Valley. Located at the southern end of San Francisco Bay, the Santa Clara Valley was undergoing a remarkable transformation during the 1960s. Both the National Aeronautics and Space Administration (NASA) and the U.S. Navy had major installations in the region and many high-technology firms were moving into the valley to support them. The influx included some of the nation's earliest manufacturers of silicon chips—small integrated electronic circuits that were beginning to replace vacuum tubes in electronic devices. Local neighborhoods teemed with electrical engineers who worked for these companies. Many of the engineers enjoyed tinkering with experiments in their basements and garages, and they were happy to answer the questions of a precocious teenager like Steve Jobs.

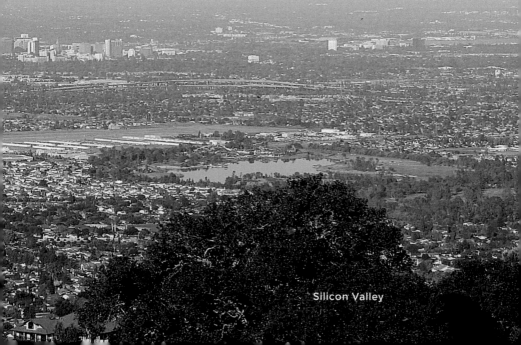

Silicon Valley

In 1968, when Steve Jobs was a freshman at Homestead High School, a mutual friend introduced him to Stephen Wozniak. Wozniak, a college freshman, was more than four years older than Jobs, but despite the age difference the two had much in common. Wozniak, who went by the nickname "Woz," loved electronics and had a penchant for practical jokes. Like Jobs, he found schoolwork dull and uninteresting, and this attitude was reflected in his grades. Woz's ultimate dream was to build a computer. At the time, computers were large, expensive machines used primarily by the military and large corporations. However, the development of silicon chips and other new technology meant that computers could be made smaller and more affordable. Woz was fascinated by the concept, and he spent countless hours drawing schematics and designing circuit boards. Steve Jobs was highly impressed with Wozniak's technical knowledge. "He was the only person I met who knew more about electronics than me," Jobs later said. Woz came away with an entirely different impression. "Steve didn't know very much about electronics," he recalled.

Whatever Jobs's technical shortcomings might have been, he more than compensated with his assertiveness. In a high school electronics class, he took on the project of building a frequency counter, an electronic device for measuring the number of times an event occurs within a specific period of time. The project required special parts, which Jobs felt a nearby electronics company might be willing to donate. But rather than submitting his request to a mere clerk or secretary, Jobs called the home phone number of Bill Hewlett, president and co-founder of the Hewlett-Packard Company. Hewlett admired young Jobs's determination, giving him not only the parts he needed, but also a summer job on the Hewlett-Packard assembly line.

Jobs (*right*) and Wozniak

In the fall of 1971, Jobs and Wozniak embarked on their first commercial venture together. An illicit phenomenon known as "phone phreaking" was taking place on college campuses and other technology hotbeds across the country. It had been discovered that the nation's long-distance telephone system could be easily manipulated with certain high-pitched tones. These signals, when transmitted across the phone line while a call was being placed, bypassed the phone company's long-distance billing system. The result was unlimited long-distance

Jobs stands in front of a photo of himself (*right*) and Steve Wozniak
working on the Apple I computer in 1976.

phone calls to anywhere in the world. Steve Wozniak read about "blue boxes"—homemade devices for producing the necessary high-frequency signals—in *Esquire* magazine and decided to try building one. He succeeded.

By this time, a sixteen-year-old Steve Jobs had landed a weekend job at an electronic parts surplus store. It was here that he first learned the art of wheeling and dealing for spare parts in Silicon Valley. Jobs could purchase the necessary components for the blue box enterprise for about forty dollars. Wozniak would then assemble the device in his dorm room. With the finished product in hand, Jobs went out in search of a buyer, typically charging $150 and splitting the profit with Woz. The scheme worked well at first but proved to be short-lived. As with any dubious moneymaking endeavor, it attracted the attention of criminals. One night while Jobs was making a sale in a dimly lit parking lot, he was approached by an armed robber. "There were eighteen hundred things I could do, but every one had some probability that he would shoot me in the stomach," Jobs remembered. "I handed over the box." Shortly afterward, Jobs and Woz decided to get out of the blue box business.

The following year, Jobs graduated from high school and prepared to go off to college. He chose Reed College, a private, liberal arts school in Portland, Oregon. The tuition was very expensive, but Paul and Clara Jobs were determined to keep their promise to Steve's birth mother. However, as had been the case in high school, the regimented schoolwork could not hold Jobs's interest and his first semester grades were abysmal. Rather than waste any more of his parents' hard-earned money, he dropped out. Jobs remained at Reed College, however, attending classes as an unregistered student and squatting in vacant dorm rooms. He could not earn credits for a degree this way, but he could study the subjects he found interesting for free. For food, he relied on the kindness of others, including a weekly meal at the local Hare Krishna temple.

Jobs entered a very experimental period in his life. By the early 1970s, America's hippie countercultural movement was winding down, but Jobs immersed himself in it. He grew a beard, dressed in ragged clothing, and adopted a vegetarian diet. He tried LSD and other mind-altering drugs. He began spending time at a commune called the All-One Farm. Jobs also took a keen interest in Eastern religions, such as Buddhism and Hinduism. He was on a search to discover who he was and what his place in the world might be. As part of this search, he took a walking tour of India. With friend Dan Kottke by his side, Jobs trekked barefoot from village to village in search of wisdom and truth. The two wanderers scrounged for food and shelter, often sleeping under the night sky. Jobs did not find the inner truth he sought in India, but he learned some valuable lessons about poverty and isolation. Most places in the world were not like affluent California.

Jobs returned to Silicon Valley with a renewed interest in electronics. Before departing for India, he had worked for video game manufacturer Atari. Once he returned, Jobs went back to his job. He also resumed his friendship with Steve Wozniak, who was now working full-time designing calculators for Hewlett-Packard. Together, they began attending meetings of the Homebrew Computer Club, a group of technology enthusiasts who were interested in building their own computers. Most of the discussion at these sessions centered

A 1976 newsletter of Homebrew Computer Club

A circuit board

on the Altair 8800, a computer kit featured in *Popular Electronics* magazine that could be ordered through the mail.

The Altair may have been the first personal computer, but it was primitive by today's standards. It had no keyboard or monitor, only switches and lights. An owner could toggle in commands to make the unit's lights blink but do little else. Steve Wozniak felt he could design a better and more useful machine. His computer would accept commands via a keyboard and use a standard television as a monitor. By the spring of 1976, his plans for the computer's circuit board were complete. Wozniak was pleased with his accomplishment but did not grasp its true potential. However, his business-minded friend certainly did. "Steve didn't do one circuit, design, or piece of code," Woz recollected. "But it never crossed my mind to sell computers. It was Steve who said, 'Let's hold them up in the air and sell a few.'" Thus, the seeds of Apple Computer Company were sown.

The HISTORY of PONG

In the fall of 1972, the world's first commercially successful video game appeared in a Sunnyvale, California tavern. Within days, people were lining up to play Pong, a crude, black-and-white version of ping-pong. A tiny, upstart company called Atari had produced the game and suddenly found itself swamped with orders for more machines. Over the next several years,

To capitalize on its success, Atari hired a small army of designers and technicians to create other video games. One of the new hires was Steve Jobs. While a good employee, Jobs's abrasive personality agitated his co-workers so much that Atari's manager arranged for him to work only at night, when he could be alone. This arrangement suited Jobs perfectly, because it meant that he could sneak his friend Steve Wozniak into the building to give him technical advice. In exchange for providing help, Woz could stay up all night playing his favorite Atari video games for free.

One day Jobs's manager approached him with a special assignment. Atari was planning a complex new video game called Breakout, in which the player uses a ball to break through a brick wall. The manager wanted Jobs to design the game's circuit board but said there were two wrinkles to the assignment. First, Atari needed the completed design immediately. Second, the circuit board needed to run on as few silicon chips as possible. In fact, if Jobs could come up with a design that used fewer than fifty chips, Atari would pay him a handsome bonus.

Jobs tried his hand at designing the Breakout circuit board alone but quickly realized it was too much for him. He called on Wozniak for assistance, promising to split the bonus should they succeed. Woz agreed, and the pair stayed up for four nights straight working on the project, a stunt that made them both sick. In the end, Steve Jobs was able to submit a design requiring just forty-two chips. He collected a bonus of $5,000, but Jobs told Woz that the bonus was only $700 and handed him half of that sum.

Woz did not learn of his friend's deception for nearly a decade. He was hurt by the lie but had no regrets about working on the Breakout project. He said it provided invaluable experience for designing Apple computers.

chapter
TWO

THE SEEDS
OF APPLE

"The most compelling reason for most people to buy a computer for the home will be to link it to a nationwide communications network. We're just in the beginning stages of what will be a truly remarkable breakthrough for most people—as remarkable as the telephone."

—*Playboy*, February 1985

In April 1976, Steve Jobs and Steve Wozniak had very modest plans for their new company, Apple Computer. They would produce and sell printed circuit boards, the copper and plastic cards to which electronic components could be attached to make a working computer. After purchasing the printed circuit board, their customers would still have to buy the various components elsewhere and assemble the machines themselves. To raise start-up money for the company, Jobs sold his Volkswagen van for $1,500 and Wozniak sold his scientific calculator for $250. They would run the operation out of the garage in Jobs's parents' home, where Jobs was still living. Neither man planned to quit his day job.

The first order came within a few days, and it was a big one. The owner of a retail electronics store called the Byte Shop wanted to buy fifty Apple computers, which he would then sell in his store. The man said he would pay $25,000, but with an important stipulation: he wanted a finished product, not just printed circuit boards without the other electronic components. Jobs and Woz were overjoyed by their good fortune, but also a bit apprehensive. Building completed circuit boards was a far more time-consuming and expensive proposition than they had envisioned.

Steve Jobs attacked the challenge with optimism and vigor. He went out and bought $15,000 worth of parts on credit. He then enlisted the help of his sister, Patty, and the friend who had traveled through India with him, Dan Kottke. The small team worked feverishly to fill the Byte Shop order. Finally, just days before the $15,000 bill for the parts was due, they finished the job. Jobs walked into the Byte Shop proudly carrying fifty fully completed circuit boards. The owner, however, was less than impressed. He thought he was purchasing finished computers, not just finished circuit boards. He was expecting each unit to have a keyboard, monitor, power supply, and so forth. Despite the misunderstanding, the owner honored the agreement and paid the bill. Jobs and Woz were ecstatic. Apple Computer was a legitimate—and profitable—business.

The two partners set about building their company. They realized that the real demand would be for fully assembled computers, not just circuit boards. Steve Jobs was the business-man, working to build the Apple name and find new clients. "I was lucky—I found what I loved to do early in life," Jobs would later say of this exciting period. Wozniak was in product development, constantly making upgrades to the Apple computer and planning an entirely new model called the Apple II.

Although the first Apple computers were superior to the Altair 8800 and other computer kits, they still left much to be desired. The Apple machines were housed in quaint wooden cases, giving them the appearance of old-fashioned typewriters or cash registers. The computer's limited output could only be displayed in black-and-white, not color. Programs had to be saved and loaded via a cumbersome process involving audio-cassettes. There were no graphics or sound. Wozniak aimed to change all that with the Apple II. The new computer would come in a sleek plastic case, have a color display with graphics and sound, and store programs on an external disk drive.

The first Apple computer, Apple I

In 1977, the average person had little interest in computers; they were bulky, mysterious devices used only by scientists, engineers, and a handful of electronics hobbyists. Few people could imagine how a computer might fit into everyday life. However, Jobs and Woz were certain that the Apple II would be a huge hit because it was different. It was easy to use, and it offered many possibilities for home and business. The two entrepreneurs imagined their computer being used in schools, libraries, offices, and living rooms. Early in 1977, Woz finished his design of the Apple II and built a working prototype. There was only one problem standing in their way: to mass-produce the Apple II, the tiny company required a large infusion of cash.

Apple II computer

Jobs realized that they needed an investor, so he scoured Silicon Valley for a bank or venture capitalist that would be willing to invest in Apple Computer and enable the company to bring its product to the marketplace. He found the going difficult. The economy was stagnant, and traditional firms had no desire to invest in two long-haired dropouts who were assembling homemade computers in their garage. Even their former employers, Atari and Hewlett-Packard, turned them down. What Apple needed was a visionary—someone who realized that success did not always come dressed in a three-piece business suit.

A man named Mike Markkula turned out to be that visionary. At age thirty-four, Markkula was not much older than Jobs and Woz, yet he was already so wealthy that he no longer needed to work. Markkula had a brief but successful career at chipmaker Intel when that company was just getting started. When Intel became a publicly traded company in 1971, Markkula made millions of dollars on the stock options he had accumulated. As a Silicon Valley veteran, he believed that people would one day want to buy their own computers, and he wanted to invest some of his wealth in this industry. When Steve Jobs approached him about buying into Apple Computer, Mike Markkula listened. He provided $92,000 and became a partner in the company. In addition to financing, Markkula brought the critical business experience that Jobs and Wozniak sorely lacked.

Computer enthusiasts got their first glimpse of the Apple II at a San Francisco electronics trade show, the West Coast Computer Faire, in April 1977. People appreciated the Apple II's stylish appearance and practical features; by comparison, all of the other computers at the trade show looked antiquated.

Within months, sales of the new model were skyrocketing. Further growth occurred when other companies began writing software specifically for the Apple II. Jobs and Wozniak had little interest in developing programs for their computers. At the time, Apple employed only two programmers, and both were high school students who came to work after their classes. As Apple-based software from other companies came on the market, the demand for Apple computers continued to grow. In particular, a rudimentary spreadsheet program called VisiCalc, introduced in 1979, showed small and midsized businesses the possible advantages of owning an Apple II. Educational institutions were also buying the computer. "One of the things that built Apple II's was schools buying Apple II's," Jobs said.

Steve Jobs began comprehending the magnitude of what he and his colleagues were accomplishing. Everything seemed to be going their way. "From almost the beginning at Apple we were, for some incredibly lucky reason, fortunate enough to be at the right place at the right time," Jobs recalled. "The contributions we tried to make embodied values not only of technical excellence and innovation—which I think we did our share of—but innovation of a more humanistic kind."

Professionally, Steve Jobs was enjoying his first taste of major success. But at home, he was desperately trying to ignore a personal crisis. Jobs's longtime girlfriend, Chrisann Brennan, was pregnant. He vehemently denied that the child was his, despite Brennan's assurances that he was the father. The couple fought fiercely over the matter. They not only lived together, but Brennan also worked at Apple on the assembly line, so it seemed they were always bickering. Some of Jobs's friends wondered how he could shirk his responsibilities as a father, just as his birth father had.

Jobs poses beside an Apple II computer in 1981.

Finally, Brennan left Apple and moved out of the house. She went to Oregon to live on the All-One Farm, the commune to which she and Jobs had belonged. On May 17, 1978, she gave birth to a baby girl. Soon after, Jobs traveled to the farm and made amends with Brennan. They named their daughter Lisa, and Jobs voluntarily began paying child support. The amicable arrangement was only temporary—before long, Jobs abruptly changed his mind, returning to his old position that the baby was not his and cutting off the support payments. A paternity test showed with nearly 95 percent certainty that Steve Jobs was Lisa's father, but Jobs continued to deny paternity. He only resumed the support payments under legal duress.

Despite Jobs's personal problems, sales of the Apple II continued to soar and within a few years the tiny company had become a major corporation. By 1980, Apple Computer employed roughly one thousand people and had annual sales of more than $100 million. In addition to its headquarters in Cupertino, California, Apple had plants operating in Texas, Ireland, and Singapore. The success of the Apple II encouraged Jobs and Wozniak to build a more powerful computer, which could be used by larger businesses. They developed a model called the Apple III, scheduled for release in the spring of 1980.

At that time, consumers made a clear distinction between business computing and home computing. They viewed "serious" computers made by technology giant IBM (or International Business Machines) as the best choice for office work, while Apple's friendly machines were better suited for playing games and balancing the family checkbook. Jobs and his associates hated the comparison. They wanted to show that Apple products could work just as well in the boardroom as in the living room. The Apple III was intended to prove this.

Apple III computer

As they worked on the new model, Apple employees began developing a reputation as tireless—almost fanatical—workers. "We were all pretty young," recalled Jobs. "The average age in the company was mid-to-late twenties. Hardly anybody had families at the beginning and we all worked like maniacs and the greatest joy was that we felt we were fashioning collective works of art much like twentieth century physics. Something important that would last, that people contributed to and then could give to more people; the amplification factor was very large."

Unfortunately for Apple, their new computer was an undeniable flop. With a price of approximately $4,000, the Apple III was more expensive than other business computers with similar capabilities. Worse yet, the machine was far too fragile and unreliable. One out of every five buyers discovered that that their brand-new computer did not work because it had suffered internal damage during shipping. Other Apple III owners were angered when their machine stopped working after just a few weeks or months. Steve Jobs was partly to blame for the problem. As head of the design team, he had insisted that the Apple III look as compact and streamlined as possible. This meant that the computer's sensitive internal components were packed too closely together for proper ventilation. To make matters worse, Jobs refused to let the engineers install an internal cooling fan, which he considered noisy and unnecessary. As a result, the Apple III tended to overheat and break down.

Although the Apple III was a costly failure, the Apple II continued to sell rapidly, with more than 30,000 units shipping each month. Wall Street business analysts looked past the Apple III setback, instead focusing on the company's startling successes. Accordingly, the initial public offering of Apple Computer stock in December 1980 was greeted with great enthusiasm. When a company goes public, it is selling pieces of ownership in the company—shares of the company's stock—to anyone wishing to buy them. Money received by the company from the initial sale of its stock is usually used to expand the business and fund new projects.

As the founders of Apple Computer, Steve Jobs, Steve Wozniak, and Mike Markkula were naturally its largest stockholders. Therefore, they had the most to gain when Apple shares became a publicly traded commodity. Jobs owned the most, with 7.5 million shares. When Apple's stock went public on December 12, 1980, investors clamored to buy shares of the revolutionary computer company, driving the price up to $29 per share. Steve Jobs was only twenty-five years old, and suddenly he was worth more than $217 million.

Many other Apple employees, who had previously received stock options as a reward for their valuable contributions to the company, also benefited. The initial public offering of Apple shares created more than forty instant millionaires. Not everyone was happy, however. Some of the company's earliest employees were excluded from the stock deal. Among them was Dan Kottke, the man who had accompanied Jobs to India and had helped construct the original Apple circuit boards. For unknown reasons, Jobs felt that Kottke and some others did not deserve to share in the wealth. Whenever they inquired about stock options, Jobs simply shrugged them off. Steve Wozniak was more sympathetic. In the months leading up to the initial public offering, he sold some of his shares to them at a reduced price, thus enabling them to receive some of the financial windfall.

Giddy with their newfound wealth, both Jobs and Wozniak splurged on luxury items. Jobs purchased a European sports car and a motorcycle. He also bought a hillside mansion but refused to furnish it. The enormous structure contained little more than a mattress on his bedroom floor and a few cherished works of art. Steve Jobs the millionaire was experiencing an internal conflict. His ongoing study of Eastern philosophies taught him that a person should live simply and concentrate on spiritual growth. Jobs still clung to those beliefs, but he now found himself tempted by the trappings of the material world.

Jobs sits in his unfurnished mansion.

He decided to use some of his financial prosperity to help others and established charities to assist blind people in India and elsewhere.

Wozniak's biggest purchase was an airplane. He bought the small, propeller-driven aircraft with the goal of becoming a licensed pilot. But he quickly learned that flying a real airplane was much more difficult than playing a video game. On February 7, 1981, Steve Wozniak crashed his plane shortly after takeoff. He and his fiancée survived but suffered serious injuries. Upon recovering, Woz decided to take a sabbatical from Apple. He married and returned to college to finish his degree. Steve Wozniak would eventually return to Apple, but he would find it a very different company.

Wholesale changes were taking place at Apple Computer in 1981. The Apple III fiasco forced the company for the very first time to lay off some of its workers. Apple's first president, Mike Scott, resigned a few months later. During this time, Steve Jobs served as chairman of the board. He may have been a co-founder, but few people other than Jobs himself believed he could lead a billion-dollar corporation. He was still very young and had no formal business training. But Jobs did have an understanding of what the average user wanted in a computer. He also had his remarkable power of persuasion. Armed with those two weapons, Steve Jobs embarked on a mission to take total control of Apple Computer.

In 1976, Steve Jobs and Steve Wozniak needed a name for their company. They talked about the idea periodically but had trouble settling on a name that appealed to them. According to Wozniak, they considered names with a technical ring, such as Executek and Matrix Electronics, but none sounded quite right.

AMING a COMPANY

One day, after visiting the commune that he loved so much, Jobs sprang a new idea on his partner. Wozniak explained, "He had just come back from one of his trips and we were driving along and he said 'I've got a great name: Apple Computer.' Maybe he worked in apple trees. I didn't even ask." The name was simple yet elegant, and it reflected Jobs's affinity for nature. Wozniak liked the name too but was concerned because it had already been taken. In 1968, the Beatles had founded Apple Records and its parent company, Apple Corps. Jobs's idea was so similar to the British music company's name that Woz worried about possible legal problems.

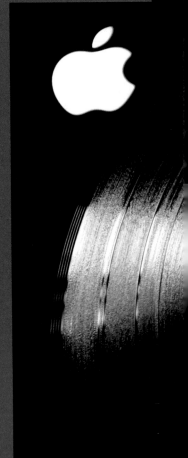

His concerns were well-founded. In 1978 Apple Corps filed a lawsuit against Apple Computer for trademark infringement. The suit was settled in 1981, when Apple Computer paid Apple Corps $80,000 and promised to stay out of the music business. That was not the end of the story, however. Over the years, as Apple introduced new music-oriented features to its computers, Apple Corps sued for breach of contract. Apple Corps usually won these battles, including a 1991 suit that cost the computer company more than $26 million.

In 2003, the British company objected to Apple's new iTunes Music Store. The case went to trial in England in 2006. This time Apple Computer won. The presiding judge reviewed the existing contract between the two companies and found that Apple was within its rights when it launched iTunes. The judge felt that because Apple Computer had merely created an online store, and was not actually producing music, there had been no trademark violation. After the ruling, Steve Jobs expressed relief that the matter was resolved, but attorneys for Apple Corps vowed to file an appeal. In 2007, the two companies announced that they had finally resolved their long-running dispute. The terms of the settlement were not disclosed.

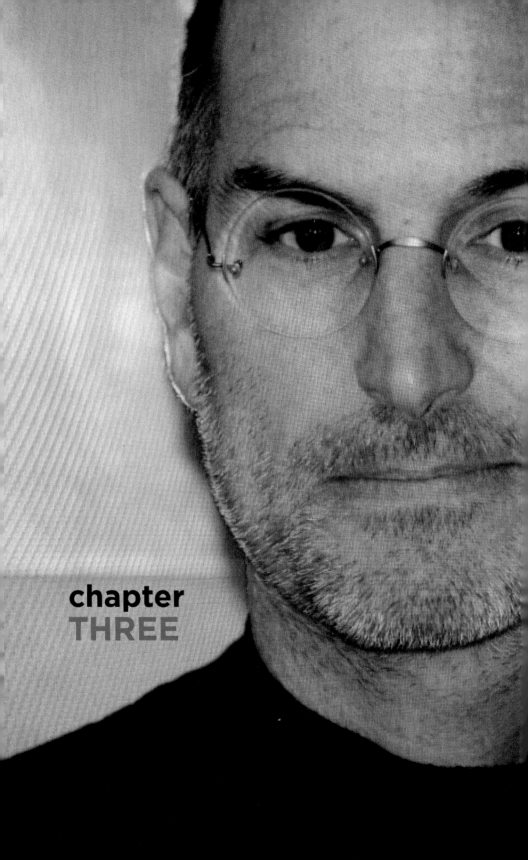

chapter
THREE

GROWING PAINS

"We think the Mac will sell zillions, but we didn't build the Mac for anybody else. We built it for ourselves. We were the group of people who were going to judge whether it was great or not. We weren't going to go out and do market research. We just wanted to build the best thing we could build."

—Playboy, February 1985

Today, everyone associates the Xerox Corporation with copiers and printers. Few people realize that in the 1970s and early 1980s, Xerox dabbled in the personal computer market as well. The company's interest in computers dated back to 1970, when it opened the Palo Alto Research Center, or PARC, in California. Xerox hired some of the brightest designers and engineers in the country and told them to create innovative electronic products that the company might someday be able to market.

Within three years, the cutting-edge PARC group had unveiled a desktop computer called the Alto. Had Xerox chosen to market the Alto, Steve Jobs and Steve Wozniak might never have bothered to start Apple Computer. But Xerox's executives felt that nobody would be interested in owning a personal computer. Like so many other Americans at the time, they had yet to grasp its usefulness and appeal. The Alto remained hidden away at PARC, and the engineers quietly continued designing radical new products.

Steve Jobs knew that groundbreaking computer work was being done at PARC, and for years he craved an opportunity to see it. When Xerox expressed an interest in investing in Apple, Jobs finally had his chance. He told the Xerox executives that they could invest $1 million in Apple, provided that they shared the secrets of PARC with him. The executives readily agreed—they still did not fully comprehend the value of PARC's inventions. A tour of the PARC facilities was arranged for Jobs and his Apple colleagues.

Computer engineers at Xerox's Palo Alto Research Center created the graphical interface technology that Jobs incorporated into Apple's computers.

When Jobs saw what the Xerox engineers were working on, he was utterly amazed. They had created a graphical user interface. Prior to this time, computers only responded to typed commands. A user typed out instructions, pressed the enter key, and watched as the computer answered with more text. The Xerox design used graphics, such as windows and drop-down menus. It was no longer necessary to remember a long list of commands. The user could instead point and click on objects with a device called a mouse. It was simple and intuitive, the type of straightforward creation that Steve Jobs loved. "It was one of those sort of apocalyptic moments," Jobs recalled years later. "I remember within ten minutes of seeing the graphical user interface stuff, just knowing that every computer would work this way some day; it was so obvious once you saw it. It didn't require tremendous intellect. It was so clear."

Jobs returned to Apple headquarters and began assembling a team for Apple's next-generation computer. He called it "Lisa," after the daughter whose existence he barely acknowledged. The Lisa would draw heavily on concepts that the PARC engineers had pioneered. It would have menu panels, overlapping windows, and scrollbars. Jobs also wanted the Lisa to have some original features. He pushed his programmers to not only recreate the PARC technology but to build upon it. As a result, Lisa's operating system contained many unique elements, such as desktop icons that launched a program when double-clicked. Icons are universal in the computer industry today, but in 1982 they were an entirely new concept.

Steve Jobs wanted the Lisa to be perfect. The Apple II had clearly been Steve Wozniak's signature project, and Jobs wanted the Lisa to be his. He infected the group with his unbridled drive and enthusiasm. Team member Trip Hawkins later recalled, "Steve had an incredible ability to rally people towards some common cause by painting an incredibly glorious cosmic objective. One of his favorite statements about the Lisa was, 'Let's make a dent in the universe. We'll make it so important that it will make a dent in the universe.'"

The Lisa finally debuted in January 1983. It was an impressive machine, weighing almost fifty pounds. Despite its bulk, the Lisa was sleek and streamlined, reflecting Steve Jobs's sense of style. The hardware possessed thoughtful features that a hard-working user would appreciate, such as a detachable keyboard. As for software, the Lisa came loaded with a full suite of programs, from word processing to drawing and graphing applications. Jobs had ensured that Lisa buyers received everything they could need, right out of the box.

Unfortunately for Jobs, his zeal proved to be the Lisa's undoing. By attempting to make the computer perfect and complete, he drove its price to astronomical heights. The original plan was to price the Lisa at $2,000. However, Jobs crammed it with so much high-end hardware and software that Apple was forced to charge a retail price of $9,995. That lofty figure vaulted Lisa out of the personal computer market. At that price the Lisa would have to compete with the elite business computer manufacturers, such as IBM, Wang, and even Xerox.

Furthermore, the Lisa was slow. Overburdened by its elaborate programming, the Lisa struggled to perform ordinary tasks. Computer enthusiasts mocked the machine with a knock-knock joke—after "Who's there?" they would wait ten or fifteen seconds before finally answering "Lisa." In the months leading up to Lisa's release, Steve Jobs confidently predicted that Apple would sell 50,000 units within the first year. He said the computer would remain a staple in the industry for a decade. In reality, Apple pulled the plug on Lisa after just two years of very disappointing sales.

Jobs poses with the Lisa computer.

With the Apple III and Lisa, the company had suffered consecutive failures. Remarkably, the six-year-old Apple II was still generating revenue, but Jobs and his colleagues knew that the product could not last much longer. Apple needed a leader who could guide the company back to success, someone with a proven record of returning wayward companies to profitability. Apple's board of directors began searching for a new president. As chairman, Steve Jobs would head the search.

Jobs's choice for the new president of Apple Computer was a man named John Sculley. At age forty-four, Sculley already had an impressive résumé. After obtaining his MBA, he had embarked on a career at soft-drink giant PepsiCo. A decade later, he became the youngest president in that corporation's long history. Sculley's specialty was marketing. The most notable demonstration of that skill was the Pepsi Challenge, a marketing campaign aimed directly at archrival Coca-Cola. In the Pepsi Challenge advertisements, consumers were shown choosing Pepsi over Coke in a blind taste test. The campaign touched off a lengthy marketing battle between the two companies that was subsequently labeled the Cola Wars.

John Sculley was apprehensive about taking the Apple job. He was comfortable at PepsiCo, and he readily admitted to himself and others that he knew very little about computers. Jobs remained adamant that Sculley was the right man for the job. The two met in New York, where Jobs dazzled the executive with his charm and charisma. At the end of the

Jobs with John Sculley

conversation, Jobs asked bluntly, "Are you going to sell sugar water for the rest of your life when you could be doing something really important?" Sculley was convinced and agreed to become the new president of Apple Computer.

Many Silicon Valley historians have since looked back on the recruitment of John Sculley and speculated about Jobs's motivations. Some believe that he intentionally sought a person he could easily manipulate, thus making Jobs the real decision maker at Apple. If so, he appeared to have made the perfect choice in John Sculley. "If you can pick one reason why I came to Apple, it was to have the chance to work with Steve," Sculley said while formally accepting the job. "I look on him as being one of the really important figures in our country in this century."

Even before the Lisa made its public debut, Steve Jobs had moved on to another project. This time, Apple was planning to create a fundamentally simple machine. The trend at Apple had been to make each new computer model more sophisticated, and expensive, than the last. Jef Raskin, a former college professor and an early Apple employee, wanted to reverse that trend. He wanted to build a computer for the average "person in the street." As Raskin envisioned it, the new computer would be lightweight, affordable, and extremely user-friendly. Raskin called his concept the "Macintosh" after a popular variety of apple (although the fruit's name is actually spelled "McIntosh"). Since the summer of 1979, Raskin had been working steadily to make the Macintosh (or Mac) a reality.

During the first few years of its existence, the Macintosh project endured constant criticism from none other than Steve Jobs. He was still focusing on the computer market's high-end corporate sector, where Apple's profit margin for each unit sold would be highest. He did not want to hear about a basic home computer that could someday sell for as little as $300. "Jobs hated the idea," Jef Raskin remembered. "He ran around saying 'No! No! It'll never work.' He was one of the Macintosh's hardest critics and he was always putting it down at board meetings."

As time passed, Jobs gradually changed his mind. He realized that Apple was not faring well in the business computer market. The company needed to get back to its roots of catering to the individual user. Further, some of Jobs's associates were blaming him for Apple's problems. They felt he was a meddler and a poor manager. With Raskin's Macintosh, Jobs could prove them wrong. He could also put his company back in the public spotlight. Rival company IBM had recently introduced its Personal Computer, or PC, and was slowly beginning to lure consumers away from Apple. If Apple did not come out with an innovative new product soon, it might be facing extinction. Although he had initially derided the Macintosh, Jobs eventually concluded that it would be Apple's savior.

Jobs energized the Mac team, much as he had done with the Lisa group, but this time to an even greater extent. Like before, he convinced the programmers and engineers that they were working on a project that would ultimately change the world. He added a sense of urgency, continually noting IBM's success at selling PCs. Finally, Jobs instilled the Mac team with boldness and arrogance. He told them that they were better than Apple's other employees, casting them as talented renegades trapped within a dull organization. Jobs compared his workers to swashbuckling pirates, with the rest of Apple serving as an unimaginative, lumbering navy. The team relished Jobs's pirate analogy. They even went so far as to acquire a Jolly Roger flag, and proudly flew the skull-and-crossbones from atop their building.

Jobs shows off an Apple MacIntosh

Privately, John Sculley and other Apple executives worried about the jealousy and tension that Jobs was fomenting within the company. During this lean period, the aging Apple II still generated most of the company's revenue. Yet Jobs's comments derided the employees of the Apple II division. Additionally, in classic pirate fashion, the Mac team raided other divisions for the best people and technology. Employees not invited to join Jobs's elite group felt snubbed, and managers deeply resented losing their best workers and programs to the Macintosh.

There were also signs of trouble from within the Mac team. Jobs made unreasonable demands of his designers and programmers, requiring that the Mac be perfect in every way. He pushed them to work ridiculously long hours, and they complied. At one point, each team member received a T-shirt that read, "90 HRS/WK AND LOVING IT." They sacrificed their personal lives out of intense loyalty to Jobs, his grand vision for the Mac, and the sense of camaraderie he had built. "He's a very motivational kind of guy, like a Roman legion commander," said a former Mac team member. "He really knows how to motivate small groups of people to produce."

Despite the heavy motivation, the team was burning out. Endless workdays, combined with Jobs's insistence on absolute perfection, were pushing people beyond their limits. Individuals learned to dread the sudden appearance of Steve Jobs at their workstation. Upon examining a person's work, Jobs would either praise it as exemplary or reject it as garbage that had to be done again from scratch. Finally, Jef Raskin sent a confidential memo to Apple's leadership. He outlined his concerns about Jobs's involvement in the project and asked for some relief. Raskin's plea went unanswered, and he eventually resigned from Apple in protest. Steve Jobs now had total control of the Macintosh.

As the project slowly drew nearer to completion, public anticipation began to build. Newspapers and magazines ran tantalizing stories about Apple's secret new computer. Internally, everyone was starting to believe that the Mac would shatter all previous sales records. Jobs stoked the flames of excitement with his wild projections, including a claim that at least 2 million Macs would sell within the first two years. The company planned a huge marketing blitz, culminating with a $1.5 million Super Bowl commercial. CEO John Sculley and Apple's board of directors were not immune to the growing Mac frenzy. Convinced that Steve Jobs was nothing short of a genius, they expanded his management authority beyond the Mac team to include an entire division. The move placed Jobs in a very powerful position.

Apple's Macintosh computer hit the shelves on January 24, 1984. The company's aggressive marketing campaign worked, as enthusiastic consumers lined up to buy the charming little machine. But after the initial rush, the Mac's monthly sales figures began to flatten out. Instead of exponential growth, Mac sales were merely trickling along. Apple's executives were at a loss to explain the disappointing numbers. They had staked the company's future on the Mac, and now it was beginning to appear as though that had been a disastrous mistake.

Even worse, Apple's workforce was fractious and divided. Jobs's controversial technique of motivating Mac team members by making them feel superior, and belittling the company's other employees, came back to haunt him. It was time to reintegrate the so-called pirates back into the navy, but neither side accepted the other. Bitter feuds broke out over salary, perks, and supervisory duties. Talented employees began leaving the company. In the executive offices, a nasty round of finger-pointing erupted. Many blamed Steve Jobs for the current debacle, saying that he had over-hyped the Mac and pushed Apple's workers to the brink of civil war. For his part, Jobs blamed John Sculley. "We're going to have to do something about Sculley," Jobs told a colleague. "He can't stay. He doesn't know what he's doing."

A fierce showdown was about to take place between Apple's president and its chairman of the board. If Jobs won, he would replace Sculley and become the unrivaled leader of Apple Computer. If he lost, he would likely be ousted from the company he had conceived and co-founded. Although he did not realize it at the time, Steve Jobs was going to lose.

BIRTH of the MAC

The release of Apple's Macintosh computer in 1984 was one of the most widely anticipated events in Silicon Valley history. Apple portrayed the Mac as a world-shattering machine that would bring computing power to the masses.

Macintosh SE with dual floppy drives

To illustrate its point, Apple produced a television commercial that aired during Super Bowl XVIII. The ad featured a bleak, authoritarian world based on George Orwell's novel *Nineteen Eighty-Four*. IBM was cast in the role of oppressive Big Brother. At the ad's conclusion, a woman wearing a Macintosh T-shirt shatters Big Brother's image with a sledgehammer. Apple's message was clear: The Mac would release consumers by giving them greater capabilities than other personal computers could.

Unfortunately for Apple, the Macintosh would need time to gain widespread acceptance, especially among software developers. Programming in the Mac's graphical user interface was a completely new experience for most software companies. Further, the Mac could not run any programs designed for IBM PCs, or even those written for other Apple computers. Accordingly, there were very few programs available for the Mac during its early existence. The initial dearth of software kept many Macintosh admirers from purchasing one.

The advent of desktop publishing saved the Mac. With its ability to manipulate text, graphics, and photos, the Macintosh was ideal for affordably producing high-quality brochures and flyers. As it became apparent that the Mac would survive and flourish, more software programs gradually became available. Throughout the 1980s and 1990s, Apple continually produced new and better models of its original Macintosh. The year 1998 saw the debut of the iMac, a stylish redesign of Apple's flagship computer, which still enjoys considerable popularity today. Much of the Mac's success can be attributed to its reputation as the trendsetter's computer, an image that Steve Jobs worked hard to propagate.

chapter
FOUR

THE NeXT MISTAKES

"I didn't see it then, but it turned out that getting fired from Apple was the best thing that could have ever happened to me. The heaviness of being successful was replaced by the lightness of being a beginner again, less sure about everything. It freed me to enter one of the most creative periods of my life."
—Stanford University commencement address, June 2005

In 1985, with his employees bickering and the Macintosh selling at just a fraction of expectations, Steve Jobs decided to make a play for complete control of Apple Computer. To succeed, he would first have to convince the company's board of directors that John Sculley, the man he had handpicked as CEO, was incompetent. Jobs would then need to persuade the board that only he could lead Apple out of the darkness that had engulfed it.

It was an enormous task to accomplish, even for someone with Jobs's powers of persuasion and influence. He met privately with a number of key figures and stated his case openly in the boardroom. Ultimately, his efforts proved unsuccessful. The consensus was that Steve Jobs's managerial style was divisive and counterproductive. Many also felt that he was largely responsible for the failure of the Lisa and the apparent failure of the Mac. On the evening of May 28, 1985, John Sculley telephoned Jobs to deliver the news. The battle was over. Jobs would be permitted to remain with the company but not in a critical position.

For one of the very few times in his life, Steve Jobs was at a loss for words. In less than a decade his two-man, garage-based enterprise had grown into a major corporation. It had made him wealthy and famous. To many Americans, Steve Jobs personified Silicon Valley. Now his own company was rejecting him. He tried to find comfort by calling a few friends, but the news was too painful to discuss. For several days, Jobs remained isolated in his home, attempting to come to grips with the reality of what had happened. Finally, he decided that he would do his best to accept his new role at Apple. Sculley had given him the title "product visionary," and Jobs figured he could at least find out what that job entailed. He was sorely disappointed.

"I was asked to move out of my office," Jobs said. "They leased a little building across the street from most of the other Apple buildings. I nicknamed it Siberia." Despite the obvious insult, Jobs was determined to press forward. He settled into his new office and called each of his former colleagues to let them know that he was willing to help in any way he could. The Apple executives were polite, but they did not offer Jobs a role in any of their projects. He continued reporting to work, but found there was very little to do. Jobs explained:

> I'd get there, and I would have one or two phone calls to perform, a little bit of mail to look at. But most of the corporate management reports stopped flowing by my desk. A few people might see my car in the parking lot and come over and commiserate. And I would get depressed and go home in two or three or four hours, really depressed.

He realized there was no future for him at Apple Computer, at least not under the current leadership. He would have to start over and try something new. Jobs began selling off large blocks of his Apple stock, leaving him with a huge cash reserve. He sold all but one share, which he kept as a symbol of the past. Next, Jobs considered what he might want to do with the rest of his life. He was only thirty years old, and he had more than enough money to last a lifetime.

Jobs thought about pursuits that would make him feel happy and fulfilled. He contemplated becoming an advocate for space exploration, going as far as asking NASA for a ride aboard the space shuttle. (NASA turned him down.) He considered politics but concluded that elected office might not suit him. At last, Jobs accepted that technology was his true calling. He would remain in Silicon Valley, and he would start a new computer company.

In September 1985, Steve Jobs officially resigned from Apple. He told the board of directors that he harbored no ill will toward the company, and he announced his plans for a new start-up. Jobs indicated that several Apple employees wished to join him in his new venture, but he assured the board that his new company would not compete against Apple. Jobs's gentle and conciliatory speech convinced the directors that he would not be seeking revenge. They asked him to remain on Apple's board, and even offered to buy 10 percent of his new business. On both counts, Jobs turned them down. He wanted a clean break.

Jobs's start-up computer company was called NeXT. The lowercase "e" stood for "education," which was the market that NeXT planned to serve. Professors, researchers, and scientists needed high-powered computers for their academic work. However, most computer manufacturers tailored their machines for either home or office use. Jobs felt that the sophisticated users in laboratories and universities were being underserved, thus creating the perfect niche market for NeXT. "We basically

Steve Jobs unveils his NeXT computer station, as Texas billionaire H. Ross Perot (*right*) looks on, in San Francisco, October 12, 1988.

wanted to keep doing what we were doing at Apple, to keep innovating," Jobs said.

The new computers would be fast, powerful, and loaded with memory. They would also be highly profitable. Silicon Valley buzzed with excitement about the extraordinary new machines that Steve Jobs planned to build. It seemed as if he might be creating another Apple, and everyone wanted to be a part of it. One investor was Texas billionaire H. Ross Perot, who bought a 16 percent stake in NeXT for $20 million. By comparison, Jobs had invested just $7 million of his own money to launch the company.

With NeXT, Jobs had precisely what he craved but was unable to attain at Apple—absolute control. The new company and its products would conform strictly to his vision. There would be no compromises or interference from others. As NeXT's employees soon discovered, the Jobs vision was sheer perfection, and he would accept nothing less. Money was no object in this dogged pursuit of the flawless organization. Jobs paid the best graphic designer he could find $100,000 to develop the company's logo. He hired a world-renowned architect to design the NeXT headquarters. As for the factory where the NeXT computers would be manufactured, Jobs insisted that it be spotless, beautiful, and fully automated. The demand for total perfection slowed all aspects of the company's progress to a crawl. During the first three years of its existence, NeXT spent tens of millions of dollars without selling a single computer.

Steve Jobs proudly introduced the first NeXT product at a gala event in October 1988. Known simply as the NeXT Computer, it was a stylish black cube containing an impressive array of hardware and software. Computer industry reporters present at the unveiling fawned over the machine's elegant shape and appearance. They wrote glowingly of its state-of-the-art specifications: a twenty-five-megahertz processor, eight megabytes of memory, and a 250-megabyte disk drive. It appeared that Steve Jobs's demands for perfection had finally paid off. Now all that remained was to sit back and wait for the orders to arrive. The sparkling, automated NeXT factory stood ready to produce as many as 120,000 machines per year.

The NeXT computer system

While building NeXT was Jobs's passion during the mid- to late 1980s, it was not his only endeavor. Several years earlier, Jobs had learned of a remarkable computer graphics team that was working for *Star Wars* creator George Lucas. The group was exploring the possibility of replacing traditional model-based special effects in movies with computer-generated imagery, or CGI. "They developed software and actually built some specialized hardware at the time," Jobs said admiringly of the graphics team. Since 1979, Lucas had poured millions of dollars into pioneering CGI technology. Although he was convinced that CGI would someday play an essential role in modern filmmaking, he was unwilling to continue funding the project. Accordingly, Lucas announced that his computer graphics division was up for sale at a price of $30 million.

Jobs was extremely interested in purchasing the CGI group and its technology. He did not want it for moviemaking, however. Jobs felt that the extraordinary graphics hardware and software could be transformed into a high-end business product. He imagined that television-marketing firms would use it to create visually stunning commercials. Hospitals could use it to enhance X-rays and MRI results. The number of potential applications for such a product seemed limitless.

Although Jobs was excited about this idea, he could not yet reveal that excitement. First, he needed to talk George Lucas into lowering the price tag. Jobs coolly negotiated with Lucas for months, gradually persuading the film producer to accept a reduced amount. In the end, Jobs purchased Lucas's computer graphics division for approximately $10 million, just a third of the original asking price. The new company adopted the name "Pixar," reflecting its mission as a manipulator of pixels. Among the roughly forty employees were several master animators and artists. Their job was to produce dazzling animated short films, which would demonstrate the capabilities of the Pixar Image Computer.

From its inception, Pixar struggled financially. A sales force spread out across the country, trying to convince hospitals and corporations that they needed a Pixar computer, but there were few buyers. Nobody doubted the computer's usefulness, but it was too complicated for the average person to operate. It was also extremely expensive. At $135,000 each, only very large organizations could afford the investment. The U.S. government purchased several units for analyzing spy satellite photos, but there were few additional sales. By 1988, Pixar had sold a grand total of 120 computers.

Unlike NeXT, where Jobs was involved in nearly every issue and decision, he allowed Pixar to operate almost independently. He viewed NeXT as his job and Pixar as his hobby. Jobs's only requirement was that the Pixar managers visit him once a month and update him on their progress. The two managers, Ed Catmull and Alvy Ray Smith, would rehearse a script of what they wanted to say during their meetings with Jobs. Their goal was to highlight Pixar's accomplishments and downplay the fact that it was losing $10 million a year. The ploy rarely worked. Pixar had no outside investors, as NeXT did. Jobs was keeping Pixar afloat entirely with his own money, and he would not be distracted from asking Catmull and Smith difficult questions. Although Jobs did not like the answers he was hearing, he refused to give up on Pixar, and continued writing checks to keep the company operating.

Pixar's financial outlook in 1989 was troubling, but NeXT's situation bordered on outright disaster. Once the initial fanfare over the NeXT cube computer faded, it became obvious that NeXT's target market—colleges and universities—were not eager to buy the machine. The NeXT Computer was sleek and sophisticated, but it lacked the raw computing power necessary for scholarly research. Powerful workstations offered by Sun Microsystems and other companies seemed better suited for the task. The cool reception that NeXT received from the academic world forced Jobs to search elsewhere for buyers. He recast the computer as a tool for business and struck a deal with a national retailer to sell the NeXT machine in its stores. Businesses were even less impressed with the cube computer than academia had been. It was a terrible failure.

Professionally, Steve Jobs was struggling—both of his companies were floundering helplessly. But his personal life was improving markedly. In the fall of 1989, he fell in love with Laurene Powell, a graduate student in the business school at Stanford University. Although Laurene was nine years younger than Steve, she shared many of his interests, including a vegetarian lifestyle, and they became constant companions. The relationship flourished for more than a year, and then

Steve and Laurene

Laurene announced that she was pregnant. For Steve Jobs, it was a replay of history. Fourteen years earlier, he had rejected a pregnant girlfriend and their unborn child. This time would be different. Laurene insisted that they marry, and after some initial hesitation, Steve agreed. The wedding took place on March 18, 1991, at Yosemite National Park. Their first child, a son named Reed, was born six months later.

Steve Jobs immersed himself in family life, using it as a shelter from his many troubles at work. NeXT and Pixar were hemorrhaging money at a combined rate of $60 million per year. He attempted to slow the bleeding by laying off more than a third of Pixar's employees. Jobs was persuaded, however, to keep the company's collection of talented artists and animators. That group's short films were receiving critical acclaim in Hollywood and around the world. Pixar had become the undisputed leader in computer animation. It seemed that nobody wanted to buy a Pixar computer, but everyone wanted to watch the cute little movies that Pixar's staff created on those computers. Jobs continued funding the animation projects, hoping that they would someday transform Pixar into a lucrative business. His patience, foresight, and persistence were about to be richly rewarded.

Steve Job's FAMILY TREE

As with many adopted children, Steve Jobs took a keen interest in learning the identity of his birth parents. Throughout his young adulthood, Jobs periodically hired private investigators in an attempt to locate them.

His efforts finally paid off in the 1980s with the discovery of his biological mother, Joanne Simpson. As it turned out, she and Jobs's natural father had stayed together, eventually marrying and moving to Green Bay, Wisconsin. A few years later they had a daughter, whom they named Mona. But the marriage was not a happy one, and by the time Mona was ten years old her father had left the family. Joanne Simpson decided to return to California and rebuild her life. She and Mona settled in the Los Angeles area, where an agent of Steve Jobs eventually contacted them.

Jobs was thrilled to meet his mother and discover that he had a sister by birth. His joy intensified upon learning that Mona was a successful novelist. "My sister's a writer!" he gleefully told a friend. Steve Jobs and Mona Simpson became very close, and he told her many details of his personal and business life. In 1996, Mona published a novel, entitled *A Regular Guy*, about a self-involved business tycoon named Tom Owens, whose fictional life closely paralleled the real life of Steve Jobs. The book painted an unflattering picture, and according to some reports, Jobs was angered and hurt by the apparent betrayal. Publicly, however, Steve Jobs and Mona Simpson denied that the novel created a rift between them, and maintained that they were still close.

Mona Simpson

Despite his success in finding his biological family, Steve Jobs never referred to himself as anything other than the son of Paul and Clara Jobs. They were the ones who raised and supported him in a loving household, Jobs asserted, and he always viewed them as his true parents.

chapter
FIVE

PIXAR SHOWS PROMISE

"If I knew in 1986 how much it was going to cost to keep Pixar going, I doubt if I would have bought the company."
—*Fortune*, **September 1995**

In 1923, two brothers named Roy and Walt Disney opened a small animation studio in Hollywood. With vivid imagination and tremendous skill, the Disneys went on to build an entertainment empire. Classic features such as *Snow White and the Seven Dwarfs*, *Pinocchio*, *Dumbo*, and *Bambi* set a gold standard for animated filmmaking that lasted more than half a century. But by 1990 the Walt Disney Company was struggling, and many of the company's executives felt that Disney needed a new approach.

Traditional animation techniques are extremely slow and laborious. Each frame must be hand-drawn and painted before it can be transferred to film. *Snow White*, for example, took scores of animators more than three years to produce. Since the 1970s, Hollywood had searched for a computerized method, but the results were always disappointing. Computer animation was too crude and blocky—no match for an artist's delicate hand. Yet Disney executives kept hearing about the high-quality animation coming out of Pixar, and they were intrigued.

In 1989, a Pixar production called *Tin Toy* won an Academy Award for Animated Short Film. The prestigious Oscar finally gave tiny Pixar enough courage to approach Disney. Pixar representatives inquired about making a one-hour television special for Disney, but the Disney executives declined. They had something bigger in mind: the world's first fully computer-animated feature film.

As Pixar's CEO, Steve Jobs would negotiate the terms of the deal with Disney. It was completely new ground for him. Jobs was a computer guru, not a movie mogul. He would have to rely on his instincts and raw business skill. A favorable Disney

Tin Toy characters

contract could save Pixar from impending financial ruin. Jobs sat down at the bargaining table with Jeffrey Katzenberg, the man in charge of Disney's feature film division.

There were many thorny issues to settle. Jobs wanted Disney to pay the movie's entire production and marketing costs. Katzenberg agreed. Jobs also insisted that the partnership last for three films, not just one as originally proposed. Again, Katzenberg agreed. In return, Katzenberg demanded that Disney should receive 87.5 percent of each film's box office revenue, plus all of the profits generated by movie-related merchandise, such as toys and games. This time it was Jobs's turn to agree. Even with a 12.5 percent revenue share, if the films were successful Pixar could earn much more money than it ever had before. When the contract was signed in May 1991, Steve Jobs found himself in the moviemaking business.

With the Disney deal successfully negotiated, Jobs turned his energy back to NeXT, allowing the Pixar staff to work independently on their movie. The idea of creating a full-length film simultaneously thrilled and frightened them. Pixar's short films were less than ten minutes long, but a feature movie would need to run for about an hour and a half. The artists and programmers had never attempted such a lengthy project and wondered if they could accomplish the task. They clearly needed a good story to tell, one that would hold the attention of children and adults alike. Pixar's previous successes had come from cleverly bringing inanimate objects to life by giving them humanlike qualities. The star of the Oscar-winning *Tin Toy*, for example, was a lovable toy drummer who faced destruction by a rambunctious baby. The animators decided to stick with this idea and develop it further.

While the engineers at Pixar worked on their film, which they had begun calling *Toy Story*, the crisis at NeXT deepened.

Despite Jobs's best efforts, the company's products failed to spark much interest among computer users. For the entire year of 1992, NeXT sold just 20,000 machines—a figure Apple could top in a single week. NeXT's shiny, state-of-the-art production facility sat idle. Several highly placed executives, sensing the end was near, departed to find work elsewhere. The company's accumulated losses were approaching a quarter of a billion dollars. Outside investors became scarce— Ross Perot lost confidence in the company and re-signed from the board in June 1991. Jobs could not afford to commit any more of his money. In February 1993, NeXT laid off 280 employees, more than half of its workforce. "I'm convinced that the only thing that kept me going was that I loved what I did," Jobs said of this dark time in his life.

Only one chance remained to save the company from bankruptcy. With NeXT, Jobs had tried to continue the trend he started at Apple. Specifically, he tried to make another Macintosh. Jobs's comput-ers were more reminiscent of expensive artwork than utilitarian machines. He failed to realize that, when it came to computers, most buyers valued a low price over aesthetics. As a result, the bland boxes produced by other manufacturers typically outsold Jobs's styl-ish machines. But the ambivalence about a computer's physical appearance did not extend to the programs it ran. Universally, users yearned for software that was stable, efficient, and easy to learn. Steve Jobs's passion for excellence had guaranteed that NeXT computers ran outstanding software. It was painfully obvious that

Jobs in his office at NeXT

NeXT could not continue as a hardware manufacturer, but as a software developer it just might succeed.

Jobs's operating system, known as NEXTSTEP, was the envy of Silicon Valley. It contained a graphical user interface (GUI) similar to the one he helped develop at Apple but with many improvements. Previously, major corporations like IBM, Compaq, and Dell had approached Jobs about installing NEXTSTEP on the computers they sold. They were desperate for an alternative to Microsoft's Windows operating system, which lagged far behind in GUI technology. Jobs turned them down. At the time, he was still convinced that NeXT would be a successful hardware manufacturer and had no intention of selling his coveted operating system to his competition.

By the early 1990s Jobs was beginning to regret that decision. In looking back at the early days of NeXT, he said, "We certainly made our fair share of mistakes, but in the end I think we should have taken a bit longer to realize the world was changing and just gone on to be a software company right off the bat." Learning from the mistakes of the past would enable him to save the company's future. After changing its name from NeXT Computer, Inc. to NeXT Software, Inc., Jobs transformed the organization into a software provider, with NEXTSTEP as its flagship product. The plan worked, and in 1994, NeXT reported a profit for the first time in its history. It was still far from the industry powerhouse that Jobs had originally envisioned, but at least the company would survive.

His other company, Pixar, had made a similar transition. Instead of selling computers, the Pixar staff was using its revolutionary graphics software to create a computer-animated feature film for Disney. But the process was not going nearly as smoothly as everyone had hoped. Disney's executives loved the *Toy Story* concept, and they heartily approved of Pixar's animation, but the film's storyline left them feeling unsatisfied. Nobody could say for certain what was wrong with the plot, only that it needed to be changed. The Pixar artists made revisions and tried again, but Disney remained unhappy. After two and a half years of struggling with the project, Katzenberg announced that he was shutting down production of *Toy Story*. The news came as a crushing blow to Steve Jobs. Pixar's future was once again in doubt.

As newcomers to the Hollywood scene, Jobs and his Pixar staff did not fully understand the situation at first. Film studios routinely halt production on a troubled project, only to resume work once all of the movie's problems have been ironed out. Disney had not given up on *Toy Story*. Rather, the studio only wanted to take a break and figure out what had gone wrong.

The plotline's main problem revolved around Woody, a toy cowboy who was the prized possession of a young boy. In the story, Woody feels threatened when a shiny new spaceman toy named Buzz Lightyear suddenly appears in the boy's bedroom. Pixar's animators had intended for Woody to be the film's protagonist, but his hostility toward Buzz Lightyear made him appear selfish and petty. To resolve this problem, the Pixar artists added some opening scenes showing Woody helping the other toys in the bedroom. The shots established Woody as the leader of the toys, thus making his anxiety over the arrival of Buzz Lightyear more understandable to an audience. Disney approved the changes, and in April 1994 *Toy Story* went back into production.

A scene from the Pixar movie,
Toy Story

Steve Jobs was not closely involved in the creation of *Toy Story*. During this time, he poured nearly all of his energy into the resurrection of NeXT. As the film drew nearer to completion, however, he began to appreciate more fully its groundbreaking nature. He also began to grasp the financial prospects it presented. In the spring of 1995, Jobs advised an interviewer to remember the title *Toy Story*, saying, "You will hear a lot about it because I think it's going to be the most successful film of this year." He was absolutely right. *Toy Story* debuted just in time for the Thanksgiving holiday and received a warm greeting in packed theaters across the country. Moviegoers had never before seen such vivid computer animation. The storyline appealed to both children and adults. In the United States, *Toy Story* earned nearly $192 million in ticket sales, making it one of Hollywood's top one hundred films of all time. Worldwide, it grossed more than $360 million.

For Jobs, the most important moment of 1995 was not the release of *Toy Story*—in August his wife, Laurene, had given birth to their second child, a daughter they named Erin Siena. Nevertheless, Pixar's box-office smash meant that the company could go public on the stock market, just as Apple Computer had fifteen years earlier. Apple's initial public offering had made Jobs incredibly rich, but he had invested a large chunk of this money in Pixar. Acquiring the animation group from George Lucas and keeping it afloat through nine lean years had cost Steve Jobs roughly $50 million. He freely acknowledged the financial heartache that Pixar had given him during those years. "If I knew in 1986 how much it was going to cost to keep Pixar going, I doubt if I would have bought the company," Jobs told a reporter. A successful public offering would allow him to recoup his investment and possibly earn a handsome profit as well. Before *Toy Story* had even hit theaters, Jobs was talking with investment firms about taking Pixar public.

Typically, the public sale of a company's stock occurs only after the company has proven its value. Financial institutions and investors first want to see a consistent pattern of profitability. For example, Apple Computer had been earning steady profits for three years before it went public. So far, Pixar's only pattern was one of consistent losses. The company had yet to turn an annual profit. All it had was a contract to make animated movies for the Walt Disney Company, and the terms of that contract gave Disney—not Pixar—most of the revenue. But in 1995 the U.S. stock market was entering a speculative period. Wall Street investors were starting to grasp how computers and the Internet were rapidly reshaping the American economy, and were anxious to own stock in the technology companies driving this digital revolution. Accordingly, they overlooked the typical requirement of proven profitability, instead focusing on a company's potential for future profits. Pixar was one of the first companies to benefit from the frenzied buying of technology stocks during the mid to late 1990s, known today as the "dot-com bubble."

Pixar had another important factor working in its favor—the persuasive and charismatic personality of its CEO. Steve Jobs touted his tiny animation company as "the next Disney," and made other bold predictions about its future. (Unlike many of the claims he made at Apple and NeXT, the Pixar forecasts proved accurate.) With the aid of his persistent lobbying, Pixar's initial public offering was scheduled for November 29,

1995, just one week after the release of *Toy Story*. Jobs hoped that the media buzz surrounding the film would spur investors into action. The clever strategy worked better than expected. Pixar's stock was given a starting price of $22 per share, but after the first day of trading the stock rose to $39 per share. Steve Jobs personally owned 30 million shares of Pixar stock, so he benefited immensely from the price surge. In a single day, he became a billionaire.

The success of Pixar proved to be well worth Jobs's time, patience, and energy. Now, the entrepreneur contemplated a way to transform NeXT into another grand success. His plan involved more than just a financial reward, however. If successful, Jobs would also rectify the mistakes of his past and make a glorious return to Silicon Valley's spotlight.

Culture Clash at PIXAR

For the first eight years of its existence, Steve Jobs paid little attention to daily activities at Pixar. His passion lay with developing NeXT Computer, and he rarely visited the small animation studio located an hour and a half to the north.

The arrangement pleased Pixar's staff and management. They knew of Jobs's tendency, first at Apple and then at NeXT, to be highly critical of his employees' work. They also knew of their benefactor's penchant for immersing himself in every detail of a project, personally making each little decision. The Pixar people were artists, and they were accustomed to performing their craft in a supportive and open environment. They had no interest in answering to a meddlesome, sharp-tongued boss.

As the Toy Story project reached its full stride, Jobs became very interested in the inner workings of Pixar. He began showing up at the studio more often. He hired a chief financial officer who would monitor the staff's progress and report directly back to him. Jobs also talked of moving the

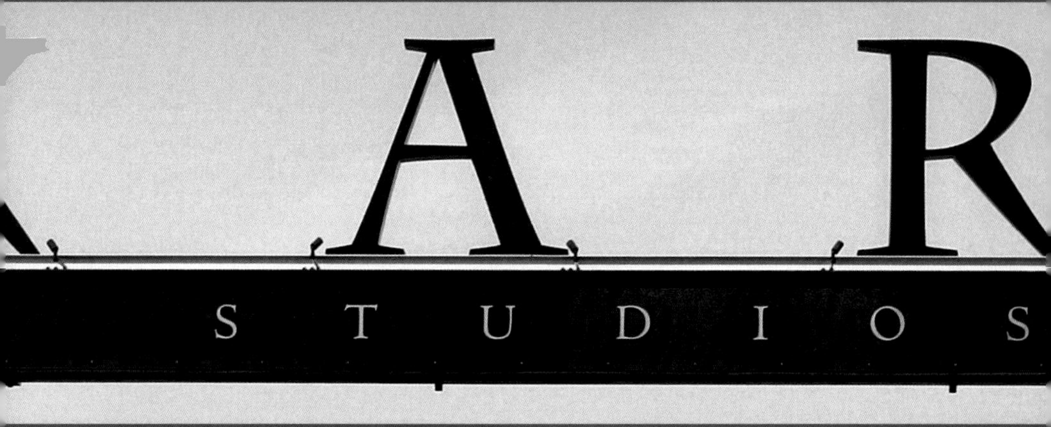
A R
S T U D I O S

chapter
SIX

RETURN TO GLORY

"You know, I've got a plan that could rescue Apple. I can't say any more than that it's the perfect product and the perfect strategy for Apple. But nobody there will listen to me."

—Fortune, **September 1995**

When Steve Jobs left Apple Computer in 1985, the company was on the verge of a renaissance. Macintosh, the machine that Jobs had virtually willed into existence, was gaining acceptance among mainstream computer users. The Mac was easy to use, with an operating system that far outstripped anything Apple's competitors could offer. When desktop-publishing software and laser printers became available, sales of the Mac soared. By March 1987, more than a million Macintoshes were humming away inside homes, offices, schools, and libraries. Jobs's vision for the machine, which he considered a work of art, had finally been realized. Only he was not at Apple to enjoy it.

The overwhelming success of the Macintosh would ultimately prove to be both a blessing and a curse for Apple. While the Mac delivered a long string of glowing earnings reports for the company, it also stifled innovation. Engineers became content to simply refine the Mac, essentially releasing modified versions of the same machine. Occasionally, the company attempted to move in a new direction, but those efforts usually lacked focus and resulted in ill-conceived products. Additionally, Apple management became preoccupied by the growing threat from Microsoft's Windows operating system. In developing Windows, Microsoft had borrowed heavily from the Mac's graphical user interface. Apple responded with a series of lawsuits, and the subsequent court battles distracted the company's leadership from its own internal problems.

From his office at NeXT, Steve Jobs observed the turmoil at his former company. Apple was gradually losing market share. The long streak of profits slowed, dried up, and then turned into losses. In 1993, Apple unveiled the Newton, a handheld device that was innovative but suffered from technical problems. Like many other Apple products of the time, the Newton failed to live up to expectations. Later that same year, an embattled John Sculley was replaced as Apple's CEO. His successor, Michael Spindler, found the job so stressful that he soon had to resign

for health reasons. The company was losing $1 billion a year, and its board of directors searched desperately for another corporation with which to merge. Nobody was interested. Talks for a potential merger with Sun Microsystems broke down after Sun realized the extent of Apple's losses.

In the summer of 1995, Microsoft released Windows 95, an operating system that rivaled—and in some ways surpassed—the capabilities of Apple's graphical user interface. If Apple had any hope to stave off bankruptcy, it would quickly need to upgrade its software to compete with Windows 95. Rather than developing a brand-new operating system in-house, Apple's new CEO Gil Amelio decided to buy an existing system from another company. Like most other Silicon Valley insiders, he admired the NEXTSTEP operating system, and it became one of the platforms that Apple considered licensing for use.

For Steve Jobs, the sudden interest in NEXTSTEP represented an extraordinary opportunity. He had barely saved NeXT from extinction, and it was obvious that while the company could survive it would never become a major player in the software industry. Apple, on the other hand, had stagnated and was in desperate need of some fresh thinking and creativity. Together, the two companies might solve each other's problems. At a meeting with executives from both organizations in November 1996, Jobs explained how NEXTSTEP would meet Apple's needs for a new operating system. Then Jobs looked Gil Amelio squarely in the eye and stated:

> If you think there's something for you in NeXT, I'll structure any kind of deal you want—license the software, sell you the company, whatever you want. When you take a close look, you'll decide you want more than my software. You'll want to buy the whole company and take all the people.

It was a tempting offer for Apple. In a single transaction, it could acquire the operating system it needed, along with a team of talented programmers to develop fresh, new products. Perhaps most important, it would bring Steve Jobs back into the Apple family, a move that would surely satisfy the company's nervous stockholders. After careful deliberation, Amelio asked

Jobs and Apple CEO Gil Amelio (*left*) speak
at a press conference held to announce
Apple's desicion to buy NeXT.

how much it would cost to purchase NeXT. Jobs told him $430 million. After some negotiating, they settled on a price tag of $377.5 million plus 1.5 million shares of Apple stock. As anticipated, the deal garnered considerable media attention—Steve Jobs was returning from exile to the company he had co-founded two decades earlier.

From the moment his return was announced, many people speculated that Jobs would soon be plotting to take over Apple again. Jobs vehemently denied these rumors. He insisted that the two biggest priorities in his life were raising his family and developing Pixar. Everything else was secondary, he said. At Apple, Gil Amelio gave Jobs the title "informal adviser," a nebulous position that carried no specific responsibilities. Jobs claimed the arrangement was fine with him. "People keep trying to suck me in," he said. "They want me to be some kind of Superman. But I have no desire to run Apple Computer. I deny it at every turn, but nobody believes me."

Jobs's public denials contrasted sharply with his actions in the hallways and offices at Apple. Upon returning, he saw a workforce that was demoralized and leadership that was confused and hesitant. The company was losing hundreds of millions of dollars each quarter, and nobody seemed to know what to do about it. Quietly, Jobs began working to foment change. A number of loyal and talented executives had come along with him from NeXT, and Jobs ensured that they took up critical positions within Apple. He spoke privately with individual board members, expressing his concerns and suggesting that Gil Amelio was an ineffective CEO. He said that Apple needed a leader with more ability in sales and marketing. The declining sales figures seemed to support Jobs's argument. Since Amelio had taken over as CEO in early 1996, Apple had lost $1.6 billion.

The losses were just one part of the story, however. Amelio was making difficult decisions that would eventually help turn the company around. By aggressively canceling unsuccessful products, and by improving the quality of successful ones, he was laying the groundwork for Apple's comeback. But huge corporations cannot reverse their fortunes overnight. A return to profitability takes months—and often years—of hard work and patience. Unfortunately for Gil Amelio, Apple's board of directors had grown tired of waiting. On July 6, 1997, they asked him to step down as CEO. Amelio felt certain that Steve Jobs had secretly orchestrated the move. "He said he didn't," Amelio complained of Jobs. "I would say that the data seems to suggest otherwise." Regardless of the cause, the fact remained that Apple Computer needed a new CEO.

The board of directors immediately asked Jobs if he wanted the job, but remarkably, he said no. "I declined, but agreed to step up my involvement with Apple for up to ninety days, help-ing them until they hire a new CEO," Jobs explained. "I agreed to be a board member, and that's all I can give. I have another life now." As before, Jobs's words did not match his actions. He used the sudden power vacuum to expand his hold on the company. He forced out other directors whom he considered either incompetent or disloyal. Among these was Mike Mark-kula, the man who had first helped Jobs and Wozniak launch Apple Computer two decades earlier. Markkula had played a part in Jobs's expulsion from the company in 1985. Now firmly in control, Jobs repaid the betrayal.

The revival of Apple would demand some unorthodox tac-tics. In August 1997, Jobs announced an unusual arrangement that shook Silicon Valley: Jobs had convinced rival Microsoft to invest $150 million in Apple. The deal was unthinkable for many loyal Apple enthusiasts, who considered Microsoft the evil oppressor of the computer world. Microsoft had stolen Apple technology to make Windows, they claimed, and then gone on to capture more than 90 percent of the operating-system market.

Jobs made his announcement at the Macworld Conference & Expo, a popular trade show for Apple devotees. As Jobs stood on stage, an enormous screen behind him projected the oversized image of Microsoft CEO Bill Gates, who was participating in the conference via satellite. To the throngs of Mac fans in attendance, the scene seemed eerily reminiscent of

Microsoft CEO Bill Gates appears on the screen behind Jobs at the 1997 Macworld Conference & Expo.

Apple's 1984 "Big Brother" commercial—except that now Jobs was announcing an alliance with Big Brother. The crowd booed loudly, and Jobs chastised them, saying that the new partnership would benefit both companies. It was undoubtedly a humbling moment for him, but it was necessary to save Apple.

Apple's tenuous financial situation forced Jobs to be conciliatory, even with former adversaries such as Bill Gates, as he tried to help the computer company turn things around. But as the head of Pixar, he could be bold and aggressive. The overnight success of *Toy Story* made Jobs a legitimate player in Hollywood. When he had first signed the contract with Disney, he was a newcomer to the film industry and the head of an

Disney CEO Michael Eisner

unproven company. Now he could bargain from a position of strength. Jobs contacted Michael Eisner, who at the time was Disney's CEO, and said that he wanted to renegotiate the contract.

In Eisner, Jobs encountered a personality much like his own. A native New Yorker, Eisner began his career at the major television networks before switching to Hollywood filmmaking. Tall and imposing, he had a reputation as stubborn and domineering, a man with whom one should not trifle. Michael Eisner had been Disney's chief executive for more than a decade when Jobs approached him. Pixar had never overly impressed Eisner. He did not initially support *Toy Story* but had allowed the movie to be made on Jeffrey Katzenberg's recommendation. Katzenberg subsequently left Disney after feuding with Eisner on other issues. Now, while staring across the negotiating table at Steve Jobs, Eisner could not deny the success of *Toy Story*. Still, he saw no reason to revise Pixar's contract.

Jobs stated flatly that the current arrangement was completely unfair to Pixar. Instead of receiving just 12.5 percent of the film revenue, Jobs argued that Pixar should share in the profits equally. He also felt that the Pixar logo should appear just as prominently as the Disney logo on all films and merchandise. Michael Eisner was aghast. He pointed out that Pixar was under contract to make two more films for Disney. Jobs acknowledged that fact but said that if Disney did not agree to more equitable terms immediately, Pixar would find a new partner as soon as the two films were completed. Eisner realized that he could not let Pixar slip away to a rival studio. Reluctantly, he submitted to Jobs's demands. A new, five-picture agreement was signed that put Pixar on equal footing with Disney. Jobs had wrestled with one of Hollywood's toughest deal-makers and won. "It took somebody of Steve's stature to get us a parity deal with Disney," commented Ed Catmull of Pixar.

Back at Apple, Jobs began a thorough review of the entire company and each of its products. He was as blunt and forceful as ever. Jobs met with the supervisors and managers of every department, challenging them to justify their team's value to the company. During the lengthy sessions, he made note of employees who impressed him and dealt directly with those people in the future. Jobs was interested only in developing products that were certain to make money. At the start of his review process, Apple had no fewer than fifty new products under development. Jobs trimmed that number to ten, keeping only those projects that showed the most promise.

There was one project in particular that intrigued him. It was a radical new computer called the iMac, which was short for "internet Macintosh." The iMac looked different from any other computer on the market. Its monitor, speakers, and central processing unit were all housed within an egg-shaped case made of colorful, translucent plastic. The typical array of cables, jacks, and ports were discreetly hidden on the iMac, giving it a sleek, streamlined appearance. Unlike other computers, the machine contained no floppy disk drive; its designers reasoned that small files could easily be transferred between computers via email. Its mouse, which was made of the same translucent plastic as the computer case, resembled a hockey puck. In addition to the iMac's unique appearance, it required little computer experience to set up or use. A first-time buyer could be surfing the Web just moments after removing the computer from its box.

Steve Jobs cherished the iMac's simplicity and its pleasing aesthetics. They were qualities he had always tried to incorporate into his computers but had been unable to do so at a reasonable price. Yet the iMac was relatively affordable at just $1,299. Jobs felt confident that he had a winner, but unlike his previous projects, he kept the iMac a secret. This time there were no outlandish sales projections or arrogant predictions about changing the universe. Jobs was so quiet about the iMac that even some Apple employees did not learn of its existence until the public unveiling in May 1998. He was learning from

Jobs unveils the iMac computer in 1998.

his past mistakes. Jobs's healthy family life no doubt contributed to this newfound attitude. That same month, he celebrated with Laurene the birth of their third child, a girl named Eve.

Sales of the new computer surpassed all expectations. In the first six weeks alone, more than a quarter of a million iMacs were sold. By the end of 1998, that figure mushroomed to 800,000. Research showed that nearly a third of iMac buyers had never before owned a computer. The friendly, colorful machine appealed to them and served as their first introduction to the digital world. For many experienced computer users, the iMac represented their first Apple product. For others, it either replaced or supplemented their old Macintosh. The iMac was a hit with a broad variety of consumers, and Apple strained to meet the demand.

In little more than a year, Steve Jobs had turned Apple around. The company went from losing money to reporting an annual profit of $309 million. Apple's board praised Jobs and again asked him to accept the title of CEO. As an incentive, they offered him 8 percent ownership in the company, but Jobs declined. Instead, he would accept only the title Interim CEO and a yearly salary of just one dollar.

As the century drew to a close, Steve Jobs could look back on a tumultuous career and call it a success. To be sure, there had been many difficult moments, but he persisted through each crisis and ultimately came out on top. As he approached middle age, it would have been easy to simply relax and reflect on the past, but that was not Jobs's nature. He still had grand designs to carry out for Apple, for Pixar, and for himself.

Restoring Apple's Polish

Steve Jobs had always understood the power of image. In the computer business, or in any business, creating quality products is merely the first step. A company must then attract consumers to those products with a clever marketing strategy. Apple Computer has always styled itself as a smart, irreverent renegade in a dull and conservative industry. By association, Apple's products have traditionally enjoyed a chic, cutting-edge image.

During Jobs's absence, Apple's many missteps gradually tarnished its image. The company's advertisements were less witty, and the products they touted were markedly less innovative. Upon his return, Jobs quickly set about restoring the polish to Apple's image. "Apple spends a hundred million dollars a year on advertising, and it hasn't done us much good," Jobs told an assembly of employees.

His first move was to re-hire the marketing firm that had produced Apple's legendary "1984" commercial. Together, they crafted a new slogan, "Think Different," which was intended to reestablish Apple's reputation as an innovator. Jobs also modernized the company's logo, replacing the garish rainbow-colored apple with an understated, pearl-white one.

A subsequent advertising campaign called "Switch" encouraged people to abandon Microsoft Windows in favor of the Macintosh and its operating system. Apple took that theme a step further with its "Get a Mac" campaign, in which two actors portray characters named "Mac" and "PC." The humorous commercials portray the Mac as cool and easygoing, while the uptight PC character is stubborn and easily confused. The successful marketing campaigns contributed significantly to Apple's resurgence as a leader in Silicon Valley.

chapter
SEVEN

iPOD AND BEYOND

"It will go down in history as a turning point for the music industry. This is landmark stuff. I can't overestimate it!"
—On the iTunes Music Store, *Fortune*, May 12, 2003

The explosion of the World Wide Web during the 1990s led to a troubling phenomenon for the music industry. Music lovers everywhere were using the Web to swap their favorite songs with each other. Of course, the sharing of music between friends was nothing new. For decades, people had made copies of records, cassettes, and CDs for one another. But that process was slow and mechanical, and it usually only occurred between acquaintances. The Internet enabled complete strangers to electronically share countless songs quickly and easily. Even worse, the scale of online music swapping was huge. Thousands, or even millions, of people could download a music file that a single individual uploaded.

The music industry was naturally alarmed. The free sharing of songs among consumers deprived record companies of profits and musicians of royalties. Though many artists viewed Internet file sharing as a vital tool to help their work reach new consumers, some others contended that online file swapping was robbing them of fair compensation for their work. The controversy made headlines in 1999, when the Napster music service went online. A nineteen-year-old college student had written the Napster software on a whim but soon found that the file-sharing program was tremendously popular with music lovers. Within months, millions of people were using Napster

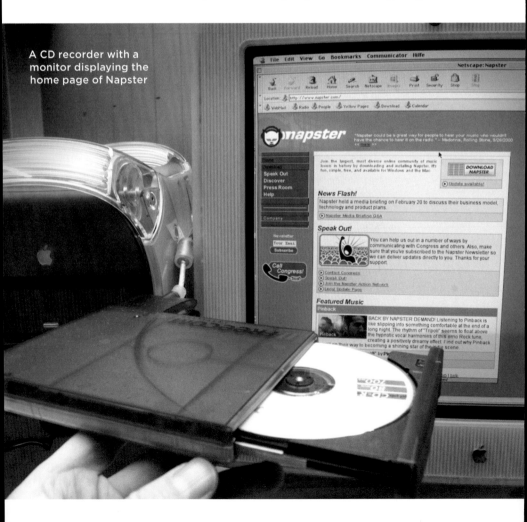

A CD recorder with a monitor displaying the home page of Napster

to exchange songs. Artists such as the heavy-metal band Metallica and rapper Dr. Dre filed suit against Napster for copyright infringement. The Recording Industry Association of America soon followed with its own lawsuit against the music-sharing service.

Ultimately, the courts shut down Napster after ruling that it had facilitated the piracy of copyrighted material. That was not the end of the story, however. The music industry had won a small victory against a single software provider, but the much larger problem of electronic file swapping still remained. Record executives were desperate for a solution. There had to be a way to allow consumers to download and listen to music digitally, but still ensure that the artists and producers who created that music received a financial reward. It was during this turbulent period that Steve Jobs approached the major music companies with an idea.

Two years earlier, in 2001, Apple Computer had introduced two new products that would revolutionize the way people accessed and listened to music. The first was a software program called iTunes, which allowed computer owners to copy songs from their CDs and play them back through the computer's speakers. Following the release of iTunes came the introduction of the iPod, a tiny yet powerful digital media player. With the pocket-sized iPod in hand, music lovers could take up to one thousand songs with them wherever they went.

Neither of these products were the first of their kind. Other companies had developed computer jukebox programs and portable MP3 players, but Apple's versions were more graceful, attractive, and refined. They also interacted perfectly together. Upon connecting their iPod to their computer, consumers could effortlessly synchronize their iPod and iTunes song playlists. At the same time, however, Apple carefully built in safeguards to prohibit file swapping and piracy.

With the iPod and iTunes, Apple had created a powerful hardware and software combination. Yet Jobs was still not satisfied. The two products could be even more dynamic, he felt, if there was an easy way for consumers to buy music online. Jobs's concept was to combine Apple's digital expertise with the vast music libraries of major record companies. Essentially, he wanted to set up an online music store where iTunes owners could download their favorite songs for a small fee. It seemed like a winning scenario for everyone involved. Consumers would relish the convenience, Apple and the record companies would share the profits, and the threat of piracy would subside.

With his typical charisma, Steve Jobs courted top record-industry executives and artists. He described for them his vision of music's future, where millions of fans paid to download a song on the same day it was released. He explained that iPods were selling faster than they could be manufactured. In short, Jobs convinced the music

The Apple iPod. After its introduction in 2001, the iPod quickly became the most popular MP3 player on the market.

industry that it was time to join the Digital Age. Even Dr. Dre, one of the earliest critics of Internet music downloading, was impressed. "Man, somebody finally got it right," he proclaimed.

The iTunes Music Store opened for business on April 28, 2003, selling an enormous catalog of songs for just ninety-nine cents each. It was an instant smash. Within the first eighteen hours, visitors purchased 275,000 songs. By the end of the year, more than 25 million songs had been downloaded from the iTunes Music Store. *Time* magazine honored the iTunes Music Store as "Coolest Invention of 2003." Its immense popularity spurred further sales of the iPod, easily making Apple's product the most popular MP3 player on the market. Before long, Apple's profits from the iPod were rivaling those of the iMac computer. The company's three music-based ventures were displaying tremendous synergy, just as Jobs had envisioned.

By this time, Jobs had finally accepted the title of CEO, formally acknowledging his intention to remain Apple's leader indefinitely. He continued to take a salary of just $1, however, saying that he needed it to qualify for the company's health plan. This was actually a long-standing custom—Jobs had never paid himself a large salary at any of his companies. He preferred compensation in the form of stock. Once Apple's financial future was secure, the board of directors rewarded Jobs lavishly. They granted him stock options for 10 million shares, which at the time had a total value of $872 million. They also gave him an extraordinary gift—his very own Gulfstream V business jet, worth more than $87 million. The directors said that Jobs had earned it.

At Pixar, the string of hit films continued. Following *Toy Story*, the studio took a chance with an animated movie about insects. *A Bug's Life* (1998) turned out to be another success.

The Pixar animators then returned to familiar ground with *Toy Story 2* (1999), a rare case of a sequel that equaled—and in some ways surpassed—its predecessor. The year 2001 saw the release of *Monsters, Inc.*, which grossed more than half a billion dollars worldwide. As before, Jobs remained outside the creative process for these films. He was Pixar's corporate leader, not an artist. Jobs would only step in if a critical business decision needed to be made. Most often, his involvement centered on Pixar's tumultuous relationship with the Walt Disney Company.

When Jobs and Disney chief Michael Eisner had originally clashed, Jobs emerged as the victor. As head of the Disney empire, Eisner resented being forced to make concessions to upstart Pixar. His bitterness set the tone for future dealings between the two companies. The problems began with *Toy Story 2*, which was initially planned as a direct-to-video release. When the decision was made to put *Toy Story 2* in theaters, Jobs asserted that it should count as one of the five feature films that Pixar was obligated to produce for Disney. Eisner disagreed, stating that *Toy Story 2* had been negotiated separately from the five-picture contract. The argument continued for some time, but Eisner refused to back down, and Jobs eventually relented.

By 2003, the Disney-Pixar contract was near its end, as Pixar was on the verge of releasing the fifth planned film, an undersea adventure entitled *Finding Nemo*. There were rumors around Hollywood that the movie, about a young clownfish and his overprotective father, was less than captivating. For Michael Eisner, a Pixar flop would not have been entirely unwelcome. Of course, Disney would lose some money in the short term, but it would also give him tremendous bargaining power for the

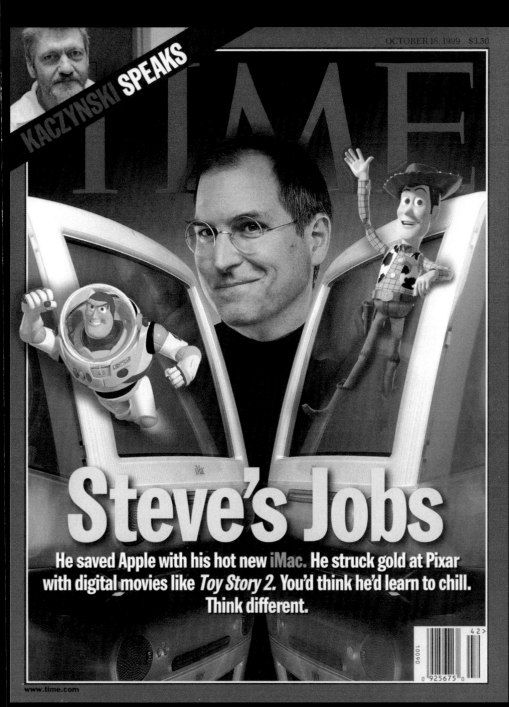

Jobs is featured on this *Time* magazine cover that depicts his role as head of two successful companies: Apple and Pixar.

upcoming contract negotiations with Pixar. When Jobs made outrageous demands, Eisner could simply point to the poor box-office figures and say no.

The opening weekend for *Finding Nemo* quickly disproved Hollywood's dire predictions, however. The movie made more than $70 million during its Memorial Day debut and went on to earn more than $860 million worldwide. *Finding Nemo* was one of the highest-grossing animated films of all time, even surpassing Disney's 1994 blockbuster *The Lion King*. Any hopes that Michael Eisner had of using *Finding Nemo* as a bargaining chip were soundly dashed. The advantage had clearly switched in favor of Steve Jobs, and he was determined to capitalize on his strong position.

The two hard-nosed negotiators met repeatedly throughout the summer and fall of 2003. Jobs was no longer content to work as equal partners with Disney. Pixar's talented storytellers and artists were doing all of the work, Jobs noted, while Disney's only contributions were in film distribution and marketing.

A *Finding Nemo* poster

Jobs felt that his company should be able to simply rent those services from Disney. The result would leave Pixar with 92 percent of the profits. Eisner considered this proposal ludicrous. "We're not for rent for anybody," he said bitterly. Jobs held a few meetings with Disney rivals in an attempt to rattle Eisner, but it did not work. Neither man refused to yield any ground.

In January 2004, Jobs made a shocking announcement that reverberated through Hollywood. "After ten frustrating months, we ended our talks with Disney," he told reporters. The negotiations had finally broken down. It appeared that Pixar would partner with another film distribution company, such as Warner Brothers or Sony Pictures. But rather than making a deal with one of those companies, Jobs merely sat back and waited. He knew that many Disney executives disliked Eisner's abrasive personality, and the company's stockholders were unhappy about declining profits in recent years. Jobs wanted to see how Pixar's abrupt departure would affect the political climate inside Disney. If there was a chance that Eisner might be replaced as CEO, Pixar could potentially benefit.

For the next six months, Jobs focused on his work with Apple and on his family. However, in June 2004 he was sidetracked from all business issues by a sudden and serious health problem. He was diagnosed with pancreatic cancer. "The doctors told me this was almost certainly a type of cancer that is incurable, and that I should expect to live no longer than three to six months," Jobs recalled. "My doctor advised me to go home and get my affairs in order, which is doctor's code for prepare to die." Later in the day, the doctors performed a procedure to examine his tumor more closely. Upon retrieving a sample of the cancer cells, they discovered something remarkable. Jobs had a very rare type of pancreatic cancer. The vast majority of pancreatic tumors are inoperable, but Jobs's tumor was among the roughly 5 percent that can be treated with surgery. The day after his operation, Jobs was e-mailing Apple's employees from his hospital bed, informing them that he was doing fine.

The brush with cancer was a particularly enlightening experience for Jobs. Just a few months after the surgery, he described his changed outlook:

> I realized that I love my life. I really do. I've got the greatest family in the world, and I've got my work. And that's pretty much all I do. I don't socialize much or go to conferences. I love my family, and I love running Apple, and I love Pixar. And I get to do that. I'm very lucky.

As Jobs recuperated, the situation at Disney gradually grew worse for Michael Eisner. The company's own films were faring poorly at the box office. Ratings at the ABC television network, a Disney subsidiary, were down. Even the company's celebrated theme parks were showing signs of sluggishness. The collaboration with Pixar had been one of Disney's few bright spots during this period. In some years, Pixar's movies had generated more than a third of Disney's film profits. Some influential stockholders openly criticized Eisner's failure to secure a long-term relationship with Pixar. They viewed it as yet another blunder by an arrogant and overpaid CEO. Among Eisner's harshest critics was Roy E. Disney, the only remaining member of the Disney family to be closely involved with the company. Roy Disney galvanized the opposition against Eisner, and soon an internal power struggle was underway.

Steve Jobs was no stranger to corporate politics. He had been expelled from his own company two decades earlier. Once an organization loses faith in its leader, there is little more to do than resign. Jobs, therefore, could not have been terribly surprised when Michael Eisner announced in March 2005 that he would step down from the Walt Disney Company. A major obstacle in the Disney-Pixar relationship had just been removed. Eisner's replacement, the new CEO Robert Iger, barely had time to move into his office before Jobs was calling to renew negotiations.

Rather than simply sign another contract, Jobs and Iger committed their companies to a much more permanent arrangement: Disney agreed to purchase Pixar for $7.4 billion. The terms of the all-stock deal ensured that Pixar would retain its own unique brand name and identity. It also ensured that Steve Jobs would not only remain involved in Pixar's affairs but would help guide the Walt Disney Company as well. The merger, which was completed in May 2006, made Jobs the single largest individual shareholder of Disney stock. He took a seat on the company's board of directors and joined a steering committee that seeks to foster innovation and creativity. Some Hollywood analysts speculated that Steve Jobs would play a significant role in rebuilding Disney's vast empire.

MUSIC REVOLUTION and CORPORATE EVOLUTION

Apple's hallmark has always been its capacity to move existing technology in new directions. The iPod is a superb example of this ability. Digital audio players were on the market for several years before Apple introduced the iPod in 2001. Yet the iPod quickly outpaced its competition and made Apple the undisputed leader in portable media devices. By the start of 2007, more than 80 million iPods were in the hands of people around the world. Users praised the iPod's compact design, its pleasing interface, and its rich, clear sound.

The iPod had a profound impact on the music industry, but it changed Apple Computer as well. Steve Jobs was still orchestrating the company's turnaround when he gambled on the slender music player. Other Silicon Valley giants had attempted to break into the lucrative consumer-electronics field and failed. Apple itself had already suffered losses in that arena, such as with its unsuccessful line of digital cameras in the late 1990s. But Jobs suspected that Apple would need to expand beyond the crowded computer market to remain profitable over the long-term, and he was correct.

In January 2007 Apple Computer formally changed its corporate name to Apple Inc. The switch reflected its ongoing growth as a technology and entertainment company, not just a computer manufacturer. It has introduced more than a dozen different versions of the iPod, from the credit-card-sized nano to larger models capable of playing video files. Through the iTunes Music Store, Apple now sells music videos, television shows, audiobooks, movies, and games. Concurrent with Apple's name change, Steve Jobs announced the iPhone—an iPod with cell-phone capabilities.

While introducing the iPhone at Macworld 2007, Jobs playfully called a local Starbucks coffee shop and ordered 4,000 lattes to go. The enduring image of Steve Jobs pacing the stage—dressed in his customary black shirt and faded blue jeans—became emblematic of Apple culture.

Jobs introduces Apple TV during his address at the 2007 Mac-World Conference & Expo.

The slim device has no keypad buttons; it consists primarily of a 3.5-inch touch screen, which can be used to make calls, surf the Web, send messages, and watch video. When the iPhone debuted in June 2007, Apple sold more than 270,000 units in the first two days alone. However, many consumers balked at the iPhone's $599 price tag, prompting Apple to reduce the cost by a third. In September 2007, the company sold its one-millionth iPhone.

chapter
EIGHT

FINAL YEARS

"Remembering that I'll be dead soon is the most important tool I've ever encountered to help me make the big choices in life. Because almost everything—all external expectations, all pride, all fear of embarrassment or failure—these things just fall away in the face of death, leaving only what is truly important. Remembering that you are going to die is the best way I know to avoid the trap of thinking you have something to lose. You are already naked. There is no reason not to follow your heart."

—Stanford commencement speech, June 2005

His cancer was back. Jobs originally believed his 2004 surgery had freed him of the disease, but it did not. Doctors found three new tumors, this time on his liver. He underwent chemotherapy, but by early 2008, the disease was taking a visible toll. He began losing weight and needed powerful medication to fight off constant pain.

During this time, disturbing new details emerged about his first cancer diagnosis, details that Jobs had tried to keep secret. He rarely spoke publicly about his health—or any element of his personal life for that matter—but when he did, he always implied that he underwent surgery shortly after diagnosis. Reporters at *Fortune* magazine learned the strange truth: Jobs had waited nine months before finally consenting to life-saving surgery. The pancreatic cancer first appeared on a routine scan of his abdomen in October 2003. His doctors advised immediate surgery, but Jobs would not consent until July 2004.

Always a firm believer in natural remedies, he wanted to explore some alternatives first. He went on special diets rich in herbs, fruits, and vegetables. He received the ancient, needle-based therapy called acupuncture. He even consulted a psychic. Friends, family, and physicians urged him to have the surgery, but Jobs refused. "I really didn't want them to open up my body, so I tried to see if a few other things would work," he explained later. After nine months, he finally realized the alternative remedies weren't going to work. Another scan showed that the pancreatic cancer was growing, and he finally agreed to have it removed surgically. Afterward, Jobs declared himself cured, and for a while that appeared to be true, but then his liver problems began.

Now, in 2008, doctors could not say if the nine-month delay had allowed the cancer to spread to his liver. The only thing they knew for certain was that Jobs needed a liver transplant, or he would die. He remained secretive about his condition, telling people that his weight loss was merely the result of the flu and other everyday ailments. Meanwhile, he quietly slipped away to Europe for experimental radiation therapies, which proved unsuccessful. In early 2009, he was forced to take another medical leave from Apple. Newspapers, business magazines, and blogs buzzed with rumors about the failing health of Apple's chief executive.

Jobs was on the waiting list for a liver transplant, and as he waited his condition rapidly worsened. An average of eighteen Americans die every day because too few people agree to donate their organs after death. It looked like Steve Jobs might become just another sad statistic, when one night he received a call from Tennessee. A young Memphis man had been killed in a car accident, and his liver was available if Jobs could get there immediately. He and his wife, Laurene, climbed aboard their jet, which streaked across the country in the middle of the night. They arrived in Memphis at 4 a.m. and proceeded directly to the hospital. For the second time in just a few years, Jobs underwent life-saving surgery.

The grueling procedure was a success, but it was only his first step toward recovery. He still needed to regain his strength, and his body needed to accept the new liver. Jobs lay in his hospital bed for weeks with Laurene by his side. He slipped in and out of consciousness and sometimes hallucinated. Despite his fragile state, he managed to complain whenever his care-givers or their medical equipment failed to meet his extremely high standards. He studied the oxygen monitor that nurses had clipped to his finger, and condemned it as bulky, complicated, and unappealing. The manufacturer should have put more thought into its design, Jobs said. Visitors and hospital staff viewed his mounting list of complaints as a sign that he was getting better. After two months, he was strong enough to fly back home to California, and three weeks after that, Jobs was working from home and making plans to return to Apple.

It was an exciting time for Apple employees, not just be-cause their iconic leader was coming back, but also because they were about to release a brand-new product: the iPad. Tab-let computers were nothing new—other companies had been making them for years—but the iPad was different. Unlike ear-lier tablets, iPad was extremely easy to use and could perform a seemingly endless variety of tasks. It looked like an overgrown iPhone, with a responsive touchscreen that enabled users to poke, swipe, and type their way through thousands of applica-tions, or apps. But it wasn't a phone. Rather, it was a powerful computer tucked into a ten-inch slab that weighed less than two pounds.

Wearing his customary black turtleneck and faded blue jeans, Jobs stepped onto a San Francisco stage in January 2010 to unveil the iPad. He still looked thin, but there was a spring in his step as he sauntered over to a leather chair and end table on the stage. He took a seat, and as the audience watched on a big screen overhead, he surfed the Web on his iPad. Jobs was happy and relaxed as he chatted his way through the demonstration. He was once again doing the work he loved most—showing off his company's latest innovative product. Consumers responded enthusiastically to the iPad, snatching up 1 million in the first month alone. It turned out to be even more successful than iPhone's launch.

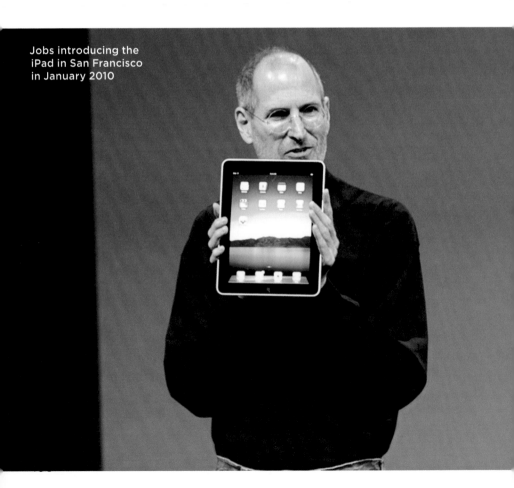

Jobs introducing the iPad in San Francisco in January 2010

Many people assumed that Apple had created iPad using the iPhone's touchscreen technology, but it was the other way around. "I actually started on the tablet first," Jobs recalled later. "I had this idea of being able to get rid of the keyboard, [and] type on a multi-touch glass display." In 2005, Apple designers transformed the idea into reality, and showed Jobs a prototype. The touchscreen worked so well that it surpassed even his expectations. "I thought, My God, we could build a phone out of this," he said. "And I put the tablet project on the shelf, because the phone was more important. And we took the next several years, and did the iPhone." Only later did he return to the tablet project, and iPad was the result. As with all successful products, Apple continued to refine both the iPhone and iPad, periodically releasing new and better versions.

In June 2010, the newly released iPhone 4 stirred controversy for Jobs and Apple. Users were complaining of dropped phone calls. At first, Jobs dismissed the complaints as petty, but when tests revealed a minor problem with the new phone's antenna, he declared, "Let's get to the bottom of this." He cut short a vacation in Hawaii, flying back to California with his teenage son, Reed. "I'm going to be in meetings 24/7 for probably two days," he told Reed, "and I want you to be in every single one because you'll learn more in those two days than you would in two years at business school."

The iPhone 4 had only a slightly higher percentage of dropped calls than did other phones, but Apple prided itself on being better than the competition, not worse. Engineers discovered that the dropped calls occurred only when users gripped the phone tightly. They recommended placing the iPhone 4 in a protective case. With Reed watching, Jobs held a press conference to explain the situation. Apple was offering free protective cases, he told reporters, and full refunds to users who were still unhappy. "We're not perfect," he grudgingly admitted. "Phones are not perfect either. We all know that. But we want to make our users happy." Ultimately, less than 2 percent of users chose to return their iPhone 4 for a refund, and it remained a popular model in the highly competitive mobile phone industry.

Jobs had initially plunged Apple into the phone business because he feared for the iPod. Phone manufacturers were starting to build music players into their devices, a development that might render the iPod unnecessary, he reasoned. Mobile phone sales were exploding, yet at the time Jobs felt most phones were clunky and difficult to use. He set out to develop an elegant phone that would gain Apple entry into this lucrative market. The iPhone achieved that goal and went on to do much more, spawning an entirely new class of smartphone and earning Apple billions of dollars in the process.

Yet Jobs was not entirely happy. He brooded over his competitors, some of whom he claimed were stealing iPhone technology. In particular, he accused Google of copying the iPhone operating system to develop its own system, called Android. Low-priced Android phones were luring some consumers away

Samsung Android

from the iPhone. "We did not enter the search business," Jobs noted, referring to Google's origins. "They entered the phone business. Make no mistake. They want to kill the iPhone. We won't let them." Jobs had Apple attorneys file a series of patent-infringement lawsuits against Android. The courts eventually found merit in some claims, but rejected others. "I'm going to destroy Android, because it's a stolen product," Jobs raged. "I'm willing to go to thermonuclear war on this."

The haughty threat was a Steve Jobs classic, reminiscent of all the passion and zeal he had shown in the past. Displays like this were becoming rare, his friends and co-workers noticed. Middle age and his health problems had mellowed him a bit. The liver transplant had bought him time, but it did not rid him of cancer. The disease was slowly spreading to other parts of his body, causing intense pain and sapping his strength. He had no appetite, and by the end of 2010 his weight dropped to a meager 115 pounds. He remained involved with the latest projects at Apple, but privately Jobs began to accept the hard fact that time was growing short.

He reflected on the past, and started thinking about his legacy. He wanted to leave behind some of the wisdom he had gained during his thirty-five-year career. That meant talking to people who could make a difference. In early 2011, President Barack Obama came to Silicon Valley for a dinner meeting with a handpicked group of industry leaders. Jobs sat beside the president and spoke with him about America's dire shortage of manufacturing engineers. More Americans needed technical training, Jobs urged, to bring back manufacturing jobs from overseas. Obama listened, and the two men spoke several more times by telephone in the following months.

Jobs spent more time at home as he continued to grow gaunt and frail, and many of his friends—and even some enemies—stopped by for a visit. Larry Page, one of Google's founders, came over to glean some insight on being a good CEO. Jobs still harbored a smoldering anger over Android, so his first impulse was to tell Page to go away, but then he reconsidered. "I tried to be as helpful as I could," he explained. "That's how I'm going to spend part of the time I have left. I can help the next generation remember the lineage of great companies here and how to continue the tradition. The Valley has been very supportive of me. I should do my best to repay."

One sunny spring day, Microsoft co-founder Bill Gates showed up to reminisce with Jobs. Once fierce competitors, they gradually acquired a mutual respect over the years. Now, these two Silicon Valley giants spoke warmly and laughed together. "We were like old guys in the industry looking back," Jobs said fondly of his three-hour chat with Gates. He made the comment to author Walter Isaacson, who was writing a Jobs biography. This was another huge change for him. In the past, Jobs had always been extremely reluctant to talk with writers about his personal life. Now that he was dying, he wanted his life experiences to be documented. It would become part of his legacy, he felt.

On August 24, 2011, Jobs went to Apple's headquarters for a board meeting. He was so weak by this time that he had to be wheeled into the boardroom in a wheelchair. As the stone-faced directors looked on in silence, Jobs read to them from a prepared letter. "I have always said that if there ever came a day when I could no longer meet my duties and expectations as Apple's CEO, I would be the first to let you know." He paused. "Unfortunately, that day has come."

Apple headquarters in Cupertino, California

The powerful words lingered as Jobs finished reading his brief statement. A cloud of somber disbelief settled over the room. Steve Jobs was the heart and soul of Apple. He had co-founded it, guided it to greatness, and then departed only to return as its savior. Nobody wanted to imagine this company without him, but now he was saying good-bye, forever. The directors showered him with their thanks and praise, and then some engineers came in to show off their latest prototypes. As always, Jobs was full of comments, criticisms, and suggestions. He fired trick questions at a new voice-recognition app called Siri and seemed pleased with its answers. When the meeting ended everyone gave him a hug, and he departed for home.

A memorial for Steve jobs outside of an Apple store in Frankfurt, Germany

Jobs spent his final weeks in the company of his family, biographer, and closest friends.

For those who knew him—even his closest friends—Jobs was always something of an enigma. They describe a man who was driven to succeed but rarely satisfied with his accomplishments. He was incredibly wealthy but seemed to place little value on material possessions. Business colleagues remember him as brilliant but also stubborn and headstrong. He was known to lavish his employees with praise in one breath and chastise them fiercely in the next. Acquaintances almost universally agree that Steve Jobs had a mesmerizing personality. With unmatched charm and persuasiveness, he could turn the harshest critic into an ardent supporter. It was an ability he had possessed since childhood.

During his early days at Apple, Jobs placed work ahead of all other considerations, including the people in his life. He wanted to change the world with computers and poured all of his energy into pursuing that goal. Later, he would gain the wisdom to realize that family was important too. "Having children really changes your view on these things," Jobs admitted. "We're born, we live for a brief instant, and we die. It's been happening for a long time. Technology is not changing it much, if at all."

Jobs died on October 5, 2011, and his death made headlines around the world. He was fifty-six years old. The following week, Apple released its latest version of the iPhone. The company that Steve Jobs had built would honor him in the best way it could— by continuing his work.

Steve,

Thanks For Cha[nging]

The World!

Cuan[g]

TIMELINE

1955   Born on February 24 in San Francisco, California.

1968   Becomes friends with electronics expert
        Stephen Wozniak.

1976   Founds the Apple Computer Company in April with
        Wozniak, and they begin assembling circuit boards in
        the Jobs family's garage.

1977   With the aid of venture capitalist Mike Markkula,
        releases the Apple II computer in April.

1978   Girlfriend, Chrisann Brennan, gives birth to daughter,
        Lisa, in May.

1980   Apple Computer becomes a publicly traded company
        in December.

1982   Takes total control of Apple's Macintosh project.

1983   Persuades PepsiCo president John Sculley to become
        Apple's CEO.

1984   Apple unveils the Macintosh in January; preliminary
        sales of the new computer fail to meet expectations.

1985   Attempts to wrest control of Apple from John Sculley;
        fails and leaves the company to found NeXT Computer,
        Inc.

1986   Purchases Pixar from *Star Wars* creator George Lucas
        for $10 million.

1989   Begins dating Laurene Powell, a graduate student
        at Stanford University.

1991   Marries Laurene Powell in March; their first child, a
        son named Reed, born in September; as head of Pixar,
        negotiates a contract with the Walt Disney Company
        to produce the world's first fully computer-animated
        feature film.

1995	Second child with Laurene, a daughter named Erin Siena, is born in August; Pixar's *Toy Story* premieres in November; Pixar goes public.
1996	Returns to Apple after that company purchases NeXT in December.
1997	Takes over as the interim CEO of Apple Computer; initiates a large-scale plan to make the company profitable again.
1998	Unveils iMac computer in May to critical and public acclaim; daughter Eve born during the same month.
2001	Apple releases the first line of iPod portable media players in October.
2003	The iTunes Music Store launched in April.
2004	Diagnosed with a rare form of pancreatic cancer in July; undergoes surgery and makes a full recovery.
2006	Negotiates the $7.4 billion acquisition of Pixar by the Walt Disney Company.
2007	In January, announces that Apple Computer is changing its name to Apple Inc., since it now produces much more than computers; also unveils the iPhone and Apple TV.
2008	Unveils iPhone 3G in June.
2009	Takes a medical leave from Apple in January; undergoes liver transplant surgery in March; returns to work in June.
2010	Introduces iPad in January; holds press conference about iPhone 4 antenna problem in July.
2011	Announces iPad 2 in March; resigns as Apple's CEO in August; dies on October 5 at age fifty-six.

SOURCES

ONE: Growing Up in Silicon Valley

p. 9, "He had a workbench . . ." Steve Jobs, interview by Daniel Morrow, Smithsonian Institution Oral and Video Histories, April 20 1995, http://americanhistory.si.edu/collections/comphist/sj1.html.

p. 10, "I'm 100 percent sure . . ." Ibid.

p. 12, "He was the only person . . ." Owen W. Linzmayer, *Apple Confidential 2.0: The Definitive History of the World's Most Colorful Company* (San Francisco: No Starch Press, 2004), 1.

p. 12, "Steve didn't know . . ." Ibid.

p. 15, "There were eighteen hundred things . . ." Jeffrey S. Young and William L. Simon, *iCon: Steve Jobs, the Greatest Second Act in the History of Business* (Hoboken, N.J.: John Wiley & Sons, 2005), 21.

p. 17, "Steve didn't do one circuit . . ." Jay Cocks, "The Updated Book of Jobs," *Time,* January 3, 1983, 25.

TWO: The Seeds of Apple

p. 22, "I was lucky . . ." Steve Jobs, "You've Got to Find What You Love," *Stanford Report*, June 14, 2005, http://news-service.stanford.edu/news/2005/june15/jobs-061505.html.

p. 26, "One of the things that . . ." Jobs, interview by Daniel Morrow, Smithsonian Institution Oral and Video Histories.

p. 26, "From almost the beginning . . ." Ibid.

p. 29, "We were all pretty young . . ." Ibid.

p. 34, "He had just come back . . ." Linzmayer, *Apple Confidential 2.0*, 6.

THREE: Growing Pains

p. 39, "It was one of those . . ." Jobs, interview by Daniel Morrow, Smithsonian Institution Oral and Video Histories.

pp. 39–40, "Steve had an incredible ability . . ." Linzmayer, *Apple Confidential 2.0*, 77.

pp. 42–43, "Are you going to sell . . ." Young and Simon, *iCon*, 93.

p. 43, "If you can pick . . ." Ibid., 94.

p. 44, "Jobs hated the idea . . ." Linzmayer, *Apple Confidential 2.0*, 88.

p. 46, "He's a very motivational kind . . ." Ibid., 95.

p. 47, "We're going to have to . . ." Young and Simon, *iCon*, 113.

FOUR: The NeXT Mistakes

p. 52, "I was asked to move . . ." Young and Simon, *iCon*, 118.

p. 52, "I'd get there . . ." Ibid., 118.

pp. 53, 55, "We basically wanted to keep . . ." Jobs, interview by Daniel Morrow, Smithsonian Institution Oral and Video Histories.

p. 57, "They developed software . . ." Ibid.

p. 61, "My sister's a writer!" Alan Deutschman, *The Second Coming of Steve Jobs* (New York: Broadway Books, 2000), 75.

FIVE: Pixar Shows Promise

p. 66, "I'm convinced that the only . . ." Jobs, "You've Got to Find What You Love."

p. 68, "We certainly made our fair . . ." Jobs, interview by Daniel Morrow, Smithsonian Institution Oral and Video Histories.

p. 71, "You will hear a lot . . ." Ibid.

p. 71, "If I knew in 1986 . . ." Young and Simon, *iCon: Steve Jobs, the Greatest Second Act in the History of Business*, 209.

p. 72, "the next Disney . . ." Peter Burrows and Ronald Grover, "Steve Jobs, Movie Mogul," *Business Week*, November 23, 1998, http://www.businessweek.com/1998/47/b3605001.htm.

SIX: Return to Glory

p. 79, "If you think there's something . . ." Young and Simon, *iCon*, 224.

p. 81, "People keep trying . . ." Linzmayer, *Apple Confidential 2.0*, 267.

p. 82, "He said he didn't . . ." Ibid., 268.

p. 82, "I declined, but agreed to . . ." Ibid., 289.

p. 85, "It took somebody . . ." Ibid., 223.

p. 89, "Apple spends a hundred million . . ." Deutschman, *The Second Coming of Steve Jobs*, 253.

SEVEN: iPod and Beyond

p. 95,   "Man, somebody finally got it . . ." Young and Simon, *iCon*, 287.

p. 95,   "Coolest Invention . . ." Chris Taylor, "The 99¢ Solution: Steve
          Jobs's New Music Store Showed Foot-Dragging Record Labels
          and Freeloading Music Pirates That There Is a Third Way," *Time,*
          November 10, 2003, 56.

p. 99,   "We're not for rent . . ." Steven Levy, "The Pixar Perplex: While
          Disney's Animation Fortunes Have Plummeted, Pixar Has
          Established a Legacy of Excellence Not Approached Since Uncle
          Walt Walked the Earth," *Newsweek,* May 26, 2003, 43.

p. 99,   "After ten frustrating months . . ." Young and Simon, *iCon*, 301.

p. 99,   "The doctors told me . . ." Jobs, "You've Got to Find What You Love."

p. 100,   "I realized that I love . . ." "The Seed of Apple's Innovation,"
          Business Week Online, October 12, 2004, http://www.businessweek.
          com/bwdaily/dnflash/oct2004/nf20041012_4018_db083.htm.

EIGHT: Final Years

p. 106,   "I really didn't want . . ." Walter Isaacson, *Steve Jobs* (New York:
          Simon & Schuster, 2011), 454.

p. 109,   "I actually started on the tablet . . ." George Beahm, ed., *I, Steve:
          Steve Jobs in His Own Words* (Chicago: B2 Books, 2011), 58.

p. 109,   "Let's get to the bottom . . ." Isaacson, *Steve Jobs*, 521.

p. 109,   "I'm going to be in meetings . . ." Ibid.

p. 110,   "We're not perfect . . ." Wilson Rothman, "Apple Gives Free
          Bumpers to All iPhone 4 Owners," MSNBC.com, July 16, 2010,
          http://www.msnbc.msn.com/id/38263228.

p. 111,   "We did not enter the search . . ." Isaacson, *Steve Jobs*, 511.

p. 111,   "I'm going to destroy Android . . ." Ibid., 512.

p. 112,   "I tried to be . . ." Ibid., 552.

p. 112,   "We were like old guys . . ." Ibid., 553.

p. 112,   "I have always said that . . ." Ibid., 558.

p. 115,   "Having children really changes . . ." Young and Simon, *iCon*, 331.

BIBLIOGRAPHY

Beahm, George, ed. *I, Steve: Steve Jobs in His Own Words*. Chicago: B2 Books, 2011.

Burrows, Peter, and Ronald Grover. "Steve Jobs, Movie Mogul." *Business Week*, November 23, 1998.

Cocks, Jay. "The Updated Book of Jobs." *Time*, January 3, 1983.

Deutschman, Alan. *The Second Coming of Steve Jobs*. New York: Broadway Books, 2000.

Elkind, Peter. "The Trouble with Steve Jobs." *Fortune*, March 5, 2008.

Hertzfeld, Andy. *Revolution in the Valley: The Insanely Great Story of How the Mac was Made*. Sebastopol, Calif.: O'Reilly Media, 2004.

Hiltzik, Michael. *Dealers of Lightning: XEROX PARC and the Dawn of the Computer Age*. New York: Harper Collins Publishers, 1999.

Isaacson, Walter. *Steve Jobs*. New York: Simon & Schuster, 2011.

Jobs, Steve. "You've Got to Find What You Love." Commencement address, delivered at Stanford University, June 12, 2005.

———. "Steve Jobs: Interview with Daniel Morrow." By Thomas J. Campanella. Smithsonian Institution Oral and Video Histories, April 20, 1995.

Levy, Steven. "The Pixar Perplex: While Disney's Animation Fortunes Have Plummeted, Pixar Has Established a Legacy of Excellence Not Approached Since Uncle Walt Walked the Earth." *Newsweek*, May 26, 2003.

Linzmayer, Owen W. *Apple Confidential 2.0: The Definitive History of the World's Most Colorful Company*. San Francisco: No Starch Press, 2004.

Markoff, John. "Apple's Visionary Redefined Digital Age." *New York Times*, October 5, 2011.

Moritz, Michael. *The Little Kingdom: The Private Story of Apple Computer*. New York: William Morrow and Co., 1984.

"The Seed of Apple's Innovation," *Business Week Online*, October 12, 2004. http://www.businessweek.com/bwdaily/dnflash/oct2004/nf20041012_4018_db083.htm.

Taylor, Chris. "The 99¢ Solution: Steve Jobs's New Music Store showed Foot-Dragging Record Labels and Freeloading Music Pirates That There Is a Third Way." *Time*, November 10, 2003.

Young, Jeffrey S. *Steve Jobs: The Journey Is the Reward*. Glenview, Ill.: Scott Foresman Trade, 1987.

Young, Jeffrey S., and William L. Simon. *iCon: Steve Jobs, the Greatest Second Act in the History of Business*. Hoboken, N.J.: John Wiley & Sons, 2005.

WEB SITES

http://www.msnbc.msn.com/id/15262121/site/newsweek

A *Newsweek* magazine interview with Steve Jobs from October 2006. The article focuses primarily on the iPod and its importance to Apple and the music world.

http://www.apple.com/education/hed/students

A page within Apple's corporate Web site that is geared specifically for students. Learn about Apple scholarships, see a list of top downloads on iTunes, and pick up computer tips and tricks.

http://www.kuodesign.com/pineapple/coverme/index.html

See the more than sixty magazine covers that have featured Steve Jobs over the years.

http://www.pixar.com

Pixar's official Web site features company news and history, a demonstration of the Pixar animation process, and previews of upcoming films.

http://www.theapplemuseum.com/index.php?id=49

Steve Jobs's biography at the unofficial Apple online museum. This site also has a wealth of information about past Apple products, including prototypes that never went into production.

INDEX

A Bug's Life (movie), 95
Altair 8800 (computer), 23
Alto (computer), 37
Amelio, Gil, 79, *80-81,* 81-82
Android phones, 110-111, *110*
Apple I (computer), *14, 23*
Apple II (computer), 22-26, *24, 27,* 30, 39, 41, 45
Apple III (computer), 28, *29,* 30, 41
Apple Inc.
    beginnings, 17, 21-22, 28
    corporate culture, 29, 44-47
    court cases, 34-35, 111
    and education, 24, 26
    growth, 28, 30-31, 33, 39-40, 43-46
    investors, 21-22, 24, 25, 38
    management, 33, 41-43, 51-53, 78-79, 81-83, 88, 95
    marketing of, 49, 89
    and Microsoft, 82-84
    name changes, 34-35, 102
    problems, 41, 47, 77-78
    reorganization of, 77-79, 81-83, 85-86
    stock options, 30-31, 71-72
Atari, 16, 18-19, 25

Brennan, Chris-Ann, 26, 28
Brennan-Jobs, Lisa (daughter), 28, 39, 59

computer animation, 60, 63-64, 68-69, 71
computer industry, 12, 25-26, 28, 39, 48-49, 53, 55-57, 66, 86, 88-89
computers, cost of, 30, 40, 58, 66, 86
computers, personal, 16-17, 23-24, 37-39, 43-44
computers and education, 55, 58-59

Eisner, Michael, 84-85, *84,* 96, 98-101

Finding Nemo (movie), 96, 98, *98*

Gates, Bill, 83-84, *83,* 112
Google, 110-111
GUI (graphical user interface), 39, 49, 57, 68, 78

Hewlett, Bill, 12

IBM, 28, 40, 44, 49
Iger, Robert, 101
iMac (computer), 49, 86, *87,* 88, 95
iPad (tablet computer), 107-109, *108*
iPhone, 102-103, *103,* 107, 111
iPod, 93-95, *94,* 102, 110
Isaacson, Walter, 112
iTunes, 35, 93-94
iTunes Music Store, 95, 102

Jobs, Clara (mother), 9, 11, 15, 61
Jobs, Erin Siena (daughter), 71
Jobs, Eve (daughter), 88
Jobs, Laurene Powell (wife), 59-60, *59,* 71, 88
Jobs, Patty (sister), 11, 22
Jobs, Paul (father), 9, 11, 15, 61
Jobs, Reed (son), 60, 109
Jobs, Steve, *8, 13, 14, 27, 32, 41, 42, 45, 54-55, 59, 66-67, 80-81, 87,*
    97, 103, 108, 114-115, 116-117
    adoption, 9, 61
    as Apple CEO, 95, 112-113
    breaks from Apple, 53, 55-57
    and cancer, 99-100, 105, 107, 111-113, 115
    character, 8-10, 12, 19, 39-40, 46, 51-53, 55, 74-75, 111, 115
    childhood and youth, 9-13, 15-16
    education, 10-12, 15-16
    interest in electronics, 11-12, 15-17
    legacy, 111, 113
    and NeXT, Inc., 53, 55, 66, 68, 71, 74-75, 79
    and Pixar, 57-58, 64-65, 74-75, 81-82
    quotes, 7, 21, 37, 51, 63, 77, 91, 105
    return to Apple, 81-82, 85-86, 88
    role in Apple, 21-22, 30, 33, 43-47, 51-53
    wealth, 30-31, 33, 71, 73

Katzenberg, Jeffrey, 65, 69, 85
Kottke, Dan, 16, 22, 31

Lisa (computer), 39-41, *41,* 43, 51
Lucas, George, 57, 71

Macintosh (computer), 43-49, *45, 48,* 51, 77
Markkula, Mike, 25, 30, 82
Microsoft Corporation, 78-79, 82-84, 89
Microsoft Windows, 68
mobile phone industry, 109-111
Monsters, Inc. (movie), 96
MP3 players, 93, 95
music industry, online, 91-95, 102

Napster, 92-93, *92*
Newton (handheld computer), 78, *78*
NeXT, Inc., 53, 55-56, 58-60, 65-66, 68, 73-74, 79, 81
NeXT (computer), *54-55, 56*
NEXTSTEP (operating system), 68, 79

Page, Larry, 112
Palo Alto Research Center, 37-39, *38*
Perot, Ross, 55, *55,* 66
Pixar, 57-58, 60, 63-65, 68-69, 71-75, 84-85, 95-96, 98-101
Pixar Image Computer, 57-58, 60, 68
Pong (computer game), 18-19, *18*

Raskin, Jef, 43-44, 46

Scotti, Mike, 33
Sculley, John, 41-43, *42,* 45-47, 51-52, 78
Simpson, Joanne (biological mother), 61
Simpson, Mona (biological sister), 61, *61*
Siri (application), 113
Spindler, Michael, 78
Sun Microsystems, 59, 78

Toy Story (movie), 65, 69, *70,* 71, 73, 84-85, 95-96
Toy Story 2 (movie), 96

Walt Disney Corporation, 63-65, 68-69, 72, 84-85, 96, 98-101
Wozniak, Stephen, 12-13, *14,* 15-17, 18-19, 21-22, 26, 28, 30-31, 33, 39

Xerox Corporation, 37-40, 40

PHOTO CREDITS